LARGEMOUTH BASS
Fly Fishing
BEYOND THE BASICS

Terry and Roxanne Wilson
Illustrated by Lefty Wilson

A Frank Amato
PORTLAND

Dedication

To the next generation of largemouth bass fly-fishermen,
especially Tyler, Kaity, Brock, and Eddie.

Frank Amato Publications, Inc.

P.O. Box 82112, Portland, Oregon 97282

503•653•8108 • www.amatobooks.com

All photographs by Roxanne Wilson unless otherwise noted.
Illustrations by Lefty Wilson
Fly Plates © Jim Schollmeyer
Book and Cover Design: Kathy Johnson

Printed in Hong Kong

ISBN: 1-57188-215-4   UPC: 0-66066-00429-1

1 3 5 7 9 10 8 6 4 2

Contents

Acknowledgments

Over several decades we've met lots of skilled and knowledgeable fishermen who have unknowingly contributed to the pages of this book. They've enhanced our understanding of largemouth bass behavior, and helped solve problems we've encountered in fly tying, equipment selection, bass locations, and fly manipulation. They've also shared our enthusiasm for largemouth bass fly-fishing and reverence for the places bass live. Interacting with them has been a special joy for us and we're grateful to each of them.

These are the special people whose efforts have made our work on this project easier and more enjoyable:

John "Lefty" Wilson, for seeing largemouth bass through a professional artist's eyes, but with a dedicated fly-fisherman's heart, and for unrelenting encouragement.

John Henry, whose tying skills accurately supplemented the flies tied by their creators, and for sharing time on the water.

Rob Woodruff, for sharing his wealth of knowledge about bass and the flies that fool them, and for guiding our efforts on his East Texas waters.

Tom Nixon, Capt. Russell Tharin, Bill Sherer, for sharing their singularly creative bass flies.

Chuck Tryon for sharing his bass fly and his perspective.

Henry Cowen, whose knowledge of bass and fly innovations he so agreeably shared.

Terry Tanner of Bass Pro Shops Outdoor World in Springfield, Missouri for sharing his tying expertise and knowledge of bass flies.

Jack Nichols, Darin Miller, and Ty Ingram, of Backcountry Outfitters in Springfield, Missouri, for their assistance and information.

Tom and Neal Conry, of Peregrine Productions, Ainsworth, Iowa, whose professional graphics abilities and advice we continually sought and utilized.

Kevin Cohenour and Phil Ames for sharing their knowledge of regional bass flies.

Dropping a fly into the pockets of lily pads is classic bassing.

Hamilton Franz, for sharing his knowledge of fishing Florida's phosphate pits.

Dana Griffin III, for giving us a different perspective on fishing clear water.

Tony Accardo, E. H. Peckinpaugh Company, Baton Rouge, Louisiana, for sharing his extensive knowledge of bass poppers and their history.

Mike Kruse, Missouri Department of Conservation Fisheries Biologist, and Wes Porak of the Florida Game and Fish Commission, for willingly answering our endless questions about biology and conservation of largemouth bass.

The Federation of Fly Fishers for providing a forum for the exchange of ideas, knowledge, and flies for largemouth bass.

Introduction

I n the prairie community of our youth, successful fishermen were elevated to a status well above their contemporaries. Some even acquired legendary status for consistently subduing larger fish. Their exploits were told, embellished, and retold. It was impossible to escape knowing about the latest gigantic fish they'd captured. From the first breath of spring until sometime past Labor Day when the local football team first trotted out upon the gridiron the discussions in the coffee shops, barber shops, the benches around the courthouse square, isles of the grocery store, and the front bench of the pool hall centered on fishing. Raised in such an atmosphere, how could a youth aspire to anything less than being one of those whose fishing exploits regularly drew praise from the local citizenry?

Those respected for catching huge catfish were bait fishermen who tightlined the Mississippi River with some secret, smelly concoctions of their own making. Those who caught largemouth bass were apt to be either bait-casters or fly-fishers, at least before spinning gear came into vogue.

We knew those most-respected fly-fishers, listened with fascination to their stories, and marveled as their fingers fashioned deer-hair bugs woven so tightly that they floated like the cork poppers we purchased at the hardware store. There were even occasional trips to a fly shop in a distant town where mother's recreational shopping was done. We imagined those who gathered there in the clutter of feathers, deer hair, and hooks to be the real experts and relished any opportunity to glean information as eavesdroppers on their conversations. Still, our own success was disappointing. We could catch bluegills, crappies, and small bass in the spring, and invariably had an encounter or two with big large-mouths, but we were always foiled by some preposterous sequence of bad luck. We sought better equipment, secret fly patterns, and more reputable waters. It helped only a little. Bass of 2 to 3 pounds became more common, but still we caught nothing like those 5-pounders with gaping, cavernous mouths displayed so proudly by our bygone heroes.

Four decades have passed since the '54 Olds first crested the hill and coasted down the blacktop to the shimmering village lake in the distance. A wrinkled janitor who befriended matriculating fishermen had spoken—no, whispered, reverently—of the huge bass he caught there. The cove was surrounded by tall bent grass, and jutting limbs draped in moss and two half-rotted stumps interrupted the shoreline. A tiny trickle parted the grass at the cove's back end and its banks gradually widened to reveal a large lake guarded by a single hickory tree on a distant hill.

Morning dew glistened in amber light contrasting with water that was clear, yet mysteriously dark and still. Thin slices of fog clung to the cattails near the cove's mouth and miniature clouds skated across the mirrored surface chased by a path of light emanating from the intense red ball on the horizon.

The tranquility was shattered by the loud splashing of surface-feeding bass. It took our breath, jump-started our hearts, and quickened our strides toward its source.

An anxious first cast, perched atop the grass two feet above the water, had to be tugged free. The yellow and black Henshall gurgled on the first gentle strip, and a swirling wake initiated by the turn of a great, unseen fish caused the puff of deer hair to lurch like a drunken surfer before it was recast to the same shade-shrouded pocket. The lake bottom exploded, and time stopped before a lifetime's biggest bass was held aloft in triumph.

Wet-wading enables fly placement under overhanging cover.

But the moment came with a heavy dose of humility from seasons punctuated by all those failed adolescent efforts and so many near misses. Like Mark Twain's attempts to give up smoking, we had quit fly-rodding for bass hundreds of times. Heck, one of us even stomped a cheap glass rod to death in frustration gone physical, but we couldn't give up our long rods because nothing, simply nothing outdoors, is as gratifying as catching largemouth bass on flies. All it takes is one. One leaping, water-churning, head-shaking, diving, tail-walking, flip-flopping, heart-stopping fight to hook you.

In these pages, we write about the nuts and bolts of largemouth bass fly-fishing. We want to pass along the knowledge we've gained through trial and error, success and frustration, luck and perseverance. In the process, we hope you'll catch a lot more bass, and a few fly rods will be spared sorry ends in the grass beside the pond.

Presenting the right fly to bass in heavy cover slants the odds in the angler's favor.

Chapter 1

Adjusting for Bass

The pursuit of largemouth bass is nothing like dropping a tiny bit of feathers on the water's surface to anticipate the delicate touch of a brightly colored fish. It's lobbing a heavy fly into weeds where it's slammed by a predator capable of jerking the rod from the angler's hands if he's unprepared for the strike. It's stripping full-sinking line from the depths, horsing the fish through brush, grabbing slack line as the bass leaps and twists above the surface. It's hanging on to the fly rod with both hands as the fighter dives for cover, pulling the bass close to remove the fly, and experiencing the joy of setting it free.

Largemouth bass are unquestionably the most sought after warmwater game fish in North America. The same compact, muscular bodies that make *Micropterus salmoides* such an efficient predator also provide it with the speed and power to fight tough, acrobatic battles. They have a remarkable ability to adapt to their surroundings and thrive in natural northern lakes, prodigious southern impoundments, sluggish bayous, and the Mississippi River. Largemouth bass are at home in weed-choked stock tanks, rock-lined millponds, and crowded city parks.

For Terry, the genesis of fly-fishing was in the spring of his twelfth year. A friend's dad had stored an aluminum-cased, 4-weight bamboo rod in the rafters of their garage. It was forbidden territory but, with dad occupied for the day, it took only a boost to retrieve the rod and the two outlaws were bicycling toward the city lake. Unable to cast conventionally, the boys adopted the bow-and-arrow method. One stood at the lakeshore holding the rod upright facing the water, while the other took the hardware-store popper to the rear and pulled the line taut before releasing the little lure. Taking turns at the rod, the team quickly captured a dozen bluegills before a series of larger swirls farther from shore distracted them. To cast that far, the rod holder would have to toe dance along a partially submerged log so the popper could be launched from the limb of a tree that overhung the water. No problem.

As the rings settled from the popper's splashdown it disappeared in a foamy explosion. A gigantic bass ripped line from the spool before the head-shaking, gill-rattling leap exposed the monster. It was easily the lake's largest aquatic resident . . . maybe a world's record. The great fish pulled for bottom amid shouts of too much advice when an audible "pop" served notice that the dried-out rod was strained beyond its limit. Momentarily horrified at the thought of the rod's demise, there was an instant of slack line and the behemoth was gone.

Reassessing the event that triggered a lifelong fascination with largemouth bass from the perspective of four-and-a-half decades provides some interesting insights. First, the humongous fish might have been 18 inches. Second, the wrong equipment was used. In that respect the two were not unlike most who try this addictive sport. Trout gear, flies, and tactics, while occasionally successful, are woefully inadequate to consistently subdue America's most popular game fish.

Nineteenth century practitioners of the fly-rodding art and outdoor writers of the period referred to largemouth bass as "green trout." Despite their lack of knowledge, they used their light-action trout rods and insect-representing flies to capture bass. Even their modest successes confirmed their uninformed notions, which then filtered through generations largely unchallenged. By the 1960s, few anglers were fly-fishing for bass. Little wonder. Deer-hair bass flies remained little changed since James Henshall's *Book of the Black Bass* was originally released a hundred years before.

The bass revolution of the 1960s was the product of bait-casters and spin-fishermen. Ray Scott's Bass Anglers Sportsman's Society sponsored tournaments in which anglers competed for large cash prizes. To gain an edge, they learned about their target species and its environment. The results were startling. Knowledge and hard work, not blind luck, were the obvious keys to success, and their ideas spread like grass fires on a windy day. The importance of water temperature and structure, the effects of weather, and many other concepts were adopted and practiced by the fishing public.

Captivated by these new ideas and methods, bass fishermen cased their fly rods and gravitated toward the proven techniques of tournament winners. A few continued to cast bass bugs in the spring, but quickly abandoned the long rod after the spawn. Amid the clamor for the latest information from the tournament trail, fly rod equipment changes lagged far behind.

In 1968 Tom Nixon published his classic work, *Fly Tying and Fly Fishing For Bass and Panfish*. The book arrived in the midst of the bass revolution, and thereby helped breathe new life into fly-fishing for bass. While Bill Dance, Jimmy Houston, and Roland Martin brought competitive bass fishing to sports pages and into living rooms, little was written about long rods and largemouths. Even articles by legendary anglers like Joe Brooks, Ray Bergman, and A. J. McClane drew minimal attention to what appeared to be a dying sport.

In the 1970s, a new voice spoke with eloquence about the pure fun of catching largemouth bass with fly rods. Dave Whitlock became the elegant spokesman that bass fly-fishing so desperately needed. The dozens of fly patterns he designed broke with tradition by replicating the bass's natural menu. He presented his bass-fishing system and demonstrated common-sense tactics that reached well below the surface where largemouth live. If Ray Scott created the bass revolution, Dave Whitlock is responsible for its fly-fishing renaissance. Respectability was restored, and the sport's following began to grow.

Slowly, with new faces singing the praises of largemouth bass and struggling for space in outdoor publications, equipment and tactics began

Bass that pursue shad schools usually belong to the same year class.

to improve. Today there are a wide selection of heavy rods, and lines designed to float, sink only the first 10 or 15 feet, or sink at a variety of rates from very slow to fast. New leaders and tippets with high tensile strength make casting heavy flies much easier, while enabling a better opportunity to fight bass successfully in the heavy cover they usually occupy.

Many bass fly-fishers choose rods and leaders that are too light and throw flies that are still nothing more than overgrown trout flies. The majority of modern bass flies, even those designed to imitate bass prey, are designed to catch fishermen, not bass. The "too-small" approach might stem from fly-fishers who own but one rod and spend their warmwater fishing time with flies that offer the possibility of catching "whatever is in the pond." A size-8 Woolly Bugger can catch some nice bluegills or redears, a crappie or two and, as a bonus, some small bass, but if the experience the angler wants is catching big largemouth bass, the same equipment would be as badly mismatched as Terry's stolen rod.

Skillful modern fly tiers create beautiful, sometimes near clones of Mr. Bass's victim list, but such flies are sometimes designed merely to display the tiers' talents. The practice can direct would-be bass enthusiasts to an unnecessarily rigid concept of bass flies. Catalogs are filled with crayfish, snake, hellgrammite, baitfish, and frog imitations. There are also lizards, worms, dragonflies, moths, and complete selections of aquatic insect life. Most look just like their natural counterparts, but bass don't really care—it's action that triggers this predator's instincts.

Making tackle adjustments accommodates the flies and techniques specialized bass fly-fishers must employ.

Bass Rods

Most of the rods we regard as powerful enough to cast the heavy, wind-resistant flies we use, as well as wrestle the real heavyweights from the toughest cover, are listed among the saltwater rods.

The qualities we seek include a powerful butt section and a rod tip designed to accelerate line speed through the casting stroke for line control. This augments both accuracy and distance. While the tightly formed casting loop, a product of rod-tip taper and timing, is much-admired and preferred in conventional situations, it's important to realize that casting an open loop is far more functional when sinking lines and heavy flies are involved.

The suitability of rod action, "fast" or "slow," is related to anglers' casting strokes, so final rod selection must be up to the individual. We can, however, recommend some specific rod qualities to test.

No one should buy a rod without casting it first. Most good fly shops provide an area for casting, as do some outdoor shows and fly-fishing conventions where rod manufacturers send their representatives with selections of rods in a variety of line weights and actions. It's important to remember, however, not to cast line only. The bass angler needs to simulate the weight and wind-resistance of the flies likely to be used with the rod. Clip the hooks of some battered veterans from the fly box and keep them handy for rod testing. A test that quickly displays a rod's inadequacies is making a few roll casts with sink-tip or full-sinking line. Bear in mind not all rods handle all situations. While most bass rods have very powerful butt sections, it's important to consider the placement of their flexibility. Those with medium action in the tip section are capable of accurately casting heavy flies and lines. For casting very wind-resistant, cup-faced poppers and deer-hair bugs with ease, an extra-fast tip is necessary. The strengths of your bass rods should be matched to their primary uses.

Serious bass fishers should choose rods in the 7 to 10 line-weight classes. Six-weight and smaller rods can provide tremendous thrills with smaller fish, but they lack the power to cast heavy flies and cannot wrench a big bass out of heavy cover.

Seven-weight outfits are preferable when we're fishing small streams and ponds. These are waters where a size-6 popper or a size-4 streamer might be good fly choices. Shorter rods, say 8 feet long, are usually better in environments with overhead brush where casting distances aren't a factor. These rods can be fairly soft and slow because the fly's weight isn't great, but some very big bass can come from small waters. The butt section should be strong enough to retain control during the fight. Shorter rods inhibit roll casts, and the use of sink-tip and full-sinking lines is often less necessary in the places short rods are customarily used. Women might prefer fast 7-weight, 9-foot rods for their ease of control. A competent caster with a good 7-weight rod can place a fly gently and silently under overhanging brush.

Eight-weight rods are the choice when windy conditions prevail, where longer casts are necessary, or when slightly heavier, more wind-resistant flies are needed. More length is desirable for this weight when float tubing or casting from a boat. In addition, the action should be considerably faster and flexibility should be confined to the tip section. A 9-foot, 8-weight rod with good butt strength and fast tip action is a good choice for the one-rod bass fisher. It's capable of fishing smaller flies as well as handling wind, distance, heavier flies, and big fish.

Nine-weight rods aren't designed to lay minute concoctions of hair and feathers gently on a still surface. Instead, they're strong, wind-busting rods capable of shooting long casts with heavy 2/0 and 3/0 flies. Most are listed with saltwater rods—the tools of the "chuck-and-duck" tactics more often associated with the salt flats. A 9-weight gets the call when we're fishing big reservoirs. Wind is a common problem, and sink-tip and full-sinking lines are the rule. We often toss big, lead-laced flies on extra-strong leaders into heavy brush or logjams. Strikes must be answered quickly, and it's imperative to winch the bass away from its tangled home on its first burst for freedom. The rod butt must be very powerful and the tip section should be fast. Rod length is important to control sinking lines; we prefer a 9-footer. We like to overload this heavy rod with 10-weight line, which causes the rod to "load up" or flex more and, consequently, cast easier because of the increased line speed.

Ten-weight rods perform the same function as 9-weights but are capable of greater distance and can overpower even the strongest bass. We know one bass guide who uses nothing but 10-weights. He told us he used one to cast to distant shad bursts and liked it so well that he now keeps three 10-weights geared with different lines and flies to be prepared for any situation. His is a 10-foot, 3-section model that has awesome power and casting distance, but handling it takes a bit of practice. The 10-weight is a saltwater rod that should be capable of short distance casting as well as punching big flies into a stiff wind.

A largemouth bass's lateral line functions like a sonar unit.

Do we recommend that bass fishermen purchase all four rod weights? No, not necessarily. If your bassing is confined to small waters you might want lighter rods. If you're a reservoir regular, heavier rods better meet your needs. For versatility on a tight budget, the one-rod bass fly-fisher should consider an 8-weight. A two-rod budget can accommodate a 7-weight and a 9-weight.

Always keep your eyes open for any new rod designs and materials that enhance your fishing. As quickly as modern technology advances, better tapers and superior materials will outdo today's rods.

Bass Reels

There are those who believe that reels suitable for largemouth bass fly-fishing should be very simple affairs because they mostly serve as line storage. Reels can, therefore, be quite inexpensive. We used to agree, but bass fishing can often demand much more than line storage. Losing the bass of a lifetime is a poor occasion to learn about the important features of good reels.

We once lost a big bass while fishing frog imitations in the bulrushes of South Long Lake in central Minnesota. That fish was missed because a cheap reel with an inadequate click drag, worn from use, couldn't prevent the spool from overrunning the fish's initial thrust for freedom. In the struggle to compensate and regain loose line, the fish found just the slack it needed to make an escape. We saw only the broad tail of the bottom-digging fish, but it could easily have been 23 inches. Clearly, a functional bass reel needs a very smooth and dependable drag.

Reels need enough spool capacity to accommodate backing. While largemouths rarely run for distant cover, backing helps fill the spool to recover more line with each revolution. During hot, humid weather, when fly lines can become soft and sticky, backing helps dry the line and prevents it from forming tight curls that make casting difficult.

These lessons finally learned prompted a serious examination of what we wanted our bass reels to do. Here's what we look for: (1) a lightweight reel that won't tire the all-day caster, (2) enough reel capacity to accommodate at least 30 yards of backing (3) a reel that enables the fly-fisher to change spools of line quickly and easily, (4) a good drag system that's smooth and easily adjustable in the heat of battle, (5) an exposed reel rim that can be "palmed" when necessary to allow a big fish to take line and instantly put the brakes on a run when the fish must be kept away from heavy cover.

There are three types of reels from which to choose: single action, multiplying, and automatics. There are lots of good choices of bass reels from very inexpensive to high dollar. The differences are largely construction material, design, and drag.

Single-action reels are easily the most popular because they offer all the features previously described without being too heavy or too complicated.

Multiplying reels offer the advantage of recovering loose coils of line quickly. Anytime the fly-fisher casts from any watercraft toward the shallows, the hooked fish tries to escape to deeper water, which often brings the fish directly toward the angler. It happens so regularly in bass fishing that a number of fly-fishers feel multiplying reels' increased cost is justified. The best recommendation for acquiring multiplying reels occurs when fishing rivers. Regardless of the current's speed, as line is stripped, loose coils trail out of control and must be gathered quickly to avoid snags.

Automatics were popular with bass fly-rodders in the 1950s and 1960s, but they have limited spool capacity, no drag adjustments, and are far too heavy, in our view, to merit serious consideration.

Reels that are fully machined from aerospace aluminum and have more technologically advanced drag systems offer lifetime guarantees and decades of trouble-free, hard use. For the serious-minded bass angler who fishes regularly, they're a good investment. Most companies that manufacture high-quality reels offer superb craftsmanship, with direct drive and anti-reverse options on some models. High-quality reel production is a very competitive field that provides the buyer with lots of choices. Buy the best reels you can reasonably afford and take good care of them.

Spare Spools

Each reel should have at least two spools, one loaded with floating line and the other with sink-tip or full-sinking line. With the means of quickly changing lines, the angler is ready to fish the surface, mid-depth, and deep sections of the water column. It really doesn't make sense to go bass fishing just with floating line. It's as self-limiting as filling your fly box only with surface flies.

Backing, Lines, Leaders, and Tippet

For backing, 30-pound-test Dacron does the job nicely. Most reels require at least a hundred yards to fill the spool so that fly lines can be recovered using fewer turns. It's a mistake to mount backing, then change fly lines several times without checking to confirm the backing is in good shape and its knots are secure.

Advanced bassers don't need lectures on the importance of using quality lines matched to their rods. We prefer line with a hard coating and internal lubrication. This enables the line to pass through the guides with less friction, which increases line speed for greater line control and distance. Specially designed lines are labeled "Bass Bug Taper," "Bug Taper" or simply "Bass Taper." The weight-forward Radical Tapers designed for pike and muskie fishing are capable of turning over the largest flies. Clear lines originally designed for use in saltwater have attracted lots of bass fly-fishers.

Sinking lines are superior to lead core sections in every way. They're much easier to pick up, cast, and maneuver in the water. Sink-tip and full-sinking fly lines are rated at inches per second (i.p.s.). Sink-tip lines can be rated as "slow" or 1.5 i.p.s. and increase to 4 i.p.s. Full-sinking line sink rates vary from 1 to 10 i.p.s. The fastest sinking lines are made for 10- to 15-weight rods. We like full-sinking lines rated for 6 inches per second to allow us to fish at mid-depth but still get the fly down quickly to deep water.

Leaders are highly adaptable tools that need to be matched to fishing conditions. They need to be as short as 3 to 6 feet on sinking lines and as long as 6 to 9 feet on floating lines. Knotless leaders are best for most largemouth waters because knots are capable of picking up silt, moss, grass, and weeds. Fluorocarbon leaders offer high-tensile strength and small diameters. That's a great advantage when fishing lightweight flies in clear water, but remember—any fish willing to ambush baby alligators, snakes, and ducklings can't be all that leader-shy when it's hungry. In addition, keep in mind most bassers use leaders that are far too light. The leader's tip needs to be stiff enough to prevent the fly from hinging on the cast. For heavy flies, the butt material should be 40- to 50-pound test to transmit the energy of the cast and turn them over efficiently. Even leaders described by their manufacturers as "bass leaders" sometimes have tips that are too light. If 16- to 20-pound-test is needed, salmon/steelhead and saltwater leaders fill the bill.

We select tapered leaders with tips that test from 8 to 20 pounds. Use as light a leader as you can, but consider its ability to turn over your fly efficiently and the abrasiveness of the cover you fish.

It can be helpful to select tippet material made by the same manufacturer as the leader to ensure the knots used to join them hold fast.

Knots

Over time, most fly-fishers develop a repertoire of knots they trust. Ours is a short list.

Join backing to fly line using an Albright knot. Its smoothness prevents it from catching on a rod guide if the fish makes a long run.

A nail knot is recommended for attaching leader to fly line. We change leaders so often, however, that tying nail knots is less efficient than permanently attached braided loops sealed with superglue. We tie surgeon's knots in leader butts with loops large enough to quickly remove or attach them and get back to fishing.

For joining leader to tippet, an ordinary blood knot works just fine. All knots pick up moss, and when we find we're removing moss too frequently we attach new tapered leaders without added tippets.

When it comes to attaching the fly, we take a simple approach. We most often use an improved clinch knot for its reliability even with large, heavy flies. A Palomar knot works well, too, but it uses up leader tips quickly. Another version of the improved clinch, the Trilene knot, can be easiest to tie correctly at dusk and when fishing at night. Its only drawback is the leader must pass through the hook eye twice, but it's easier to see shiny metal than monofilament in dim light. Instructions for it can be found in the second edition of *Guide to Fly Fishing Knots* by Larry V. Notley.

Split Shot

We've avoided using split shot for instantly added weight on our flies and leader tips because we were convinced the practice weakens leaders and adversely affects fly action. Yet we acknowledge there are times when getting a foot or two deeper while maintaining the same retrieve speed is necessary. East Texas fly-fishing guide, Rob Woodruff, uses two split shot arrangements that work with no negative effects. "For small split shot, say BB size, you can add the weight right at the knot connecting the tippet to the fly. If you need more weight to get the fly deeper, you can add larger split shot at the point where the fly line is attached to the leader." There's no hinging effect either on the cast or on the retrieve, and fly action is unaffected. Adding split shot where leader strength is greatest reduces breakage.

Stripping Baskets

Float tubes have built-in mesh aprons that serve as places for loose fly lines, but bank stalkers must cope with grass, weeds, and even pantlegs that grab lines and spoil casts. Although carpeted boats offer plenty of dry space, stepping on fly line does nothing for its useful life. Boats also have lots of gizmos and fittings for lines to wrap around. Stripping baskets make sense if you're comfortable with using them.

The Past, Present, and Future of Bass Flies

The earliest records of fly-fishing for bass in America show flies were simply enlarged versions of classic trout patterns. Professor, Parmachene Belle, Montreal, and others were tied as large as size-1/0 for bass. By the turn of the twentieth century, these enlarged trout patterns were called "lake wet flies" or "bass flies." None were constructed to look anything like any living creature; they were simply beautiful creations thought to attract bass because of their bright colors. The same concept was used in the development of patterns for landlocked salmon. Curiously, some patterns were considered only for salmon while others became known for bass despite obvious similarities between the two. The term "lake flies," then became the reference for salmon flies. Dr. James A. Henshall's classic work, *Book of the Black Bass*, published in 1881, popularized his winged deer-hair creations, appropriately called Henshall Bugs. Many regard them as the first true bass fly patterns.

Sometime before 1910, a brick mason from Chattanooga, Tennessee, Ernest H. Peckinpaugh, created the first cork-bodied bass bug. According to Tony Accardo, who bought the Peckinpaugh Company and moved it to Baton Rouge, Louisiana, "Peck opened his thermos and, in the process, dropped the cork stopper onto the water. Before he could retrieve it a bass came up and hit it." Peckinpaugh affixed some chicken feathers and embedded a double hook and returned to the lake. It was an instant success with the bass and Peck continued to tie his new creation in many colors of feathers and bucktail.

By 1914 Europe was embroiled in the conflict which eventually immersed nearly all of civilization in World War I. That ended Peck's construction of the double-hooked cork bugs. Accardo continues, "The double-hooked cork bugs he had been using were made in England, and he wasn't able to get more, so he turned his attention to building the bugs on single hooks." Still, Peckinpaugh wasn't inclined to market the new bugs. Their first distribution came about because Peck needed to trade for some additional fishing equipment.

B. F. Wilder obtained several and impressed guides throughout the East before passing some along to Will H. Dilg, a Chicago outdoor writer who quickly duplicated Wilder's success and contacted a Chicago fly tier, Cal McCarthy, to keep his fly boxes filled. Together, Dilg and McCarthy developed numerous effective color patterns that became known as the Mississippi River patterns.

Dilg is responsible for popularizing the new bugs. Numerous magazine articles proclaimed their effectiveness and created the market for them. The E. H. Peckinpaugh Company was born in 1920 and quickly took the lead in the burgeoning fishing tackle business.

Unfortunately, bass-fly development virtually came to a standstill for the next 50 or more years. As late as 1970 fly-fishing guru, Joe Brooks, in the seventh edition of his comprehensive book, *The Complete Book of Fly Fishing,* wrote, " A favorite fly for largemouth bass is the Professor, which can be used with or without a spinner." This stagnation was simultaneous to, and to some extent caused by, the bait-casting and spinning popularity explosion. Only Tom Nixon said anything new regarding bass flies. He created his Calcasieu Pig Boat in 1950. Its many-tentacled appearance admittedly copied the lures used so successfully by bait-casters. Finally, we see acknowledgement that the hardware flingers were catching fish and onto something. He also wrote about fly-casting plastic worms, which was accepted with the same enthusiasm as a visit of undetermined length by an unemployed brother-in-law.

Slowly, in the 1970s and 1980s, bass-fly design began to change with an emphasis on replicating the species' myriad food sources. Lots of people deserve credit for the changes, but none more than Dave Whitlock, who created realistic-appearing patterns such as Whitlock's Mouserat, Dave's Frog Diver, Near Nuff Frog, Wigglelegs Frog, Water Snake Diver, Hare Waterpup, Hare Worm, Hare Diver, Hare Jig Fly,

Deep Sheep Crappie, Hare Grub, a series of match-the-minnows, Matuka Sculpin, Multicolor Muddler, Sheep Shad, Sheep Sunfish, Bass Hopper, Whit's Damsel, Whit's Spent Krystal Dragon, Damsel Nymph, Dragon Nymph, and others. In the process Dave became the nation's leading bass fly tier.

Add to Whitlock's enormous contribution the work of creative tiers, such as Bob Clouser, Larry Dahlberg, Joe Messinger, Jimmy Nix, Jim Stewart, and Bob Popovics. Along with other innovative tiers, they advanced the design and effectiveness of bass flies.

Despite elevating bass flies into their own recognized category with appropriate sizes, colors, and realistic appearances, bass-fly development has lots of room for improvement. We need to stay firmly focused on action as the key ingredient of the next generation of bass flies that's sure to come in the twenty-first century. Newly developed materials and a basic understanding of duplicating the observed action of real bass prey will almost certainly spark the creativity of many innovative fly tiers now, and in the immediate future. We can create better bass flies by understanding the physical makeup of largemouth bass, especially what they see and hear. Action, more than realistic looks, is the key.

All flies, perhaps, but certainly flies for bass, should be regarded as situational. Only shallow, aggressive pre-spawn bass are apt to strike anything that invades their realm. Beyond that, we need to understand where bass are most likely to be located under a precise set of circumstances (water temperature, sunlight penetration, water clarity, prey availability, etc.) and how they could be expected to react in that environment. It's ludicrous, for example, to chug a popper across the surface while most of the bass are hiding from the midday sun and high water temperatures in depths of 20 feet. We need to design bass flies that not only duplicate the action but also suit the various situations in which bass locate under different daily and seasonal circumstances. No fly is, or will become, a panacea. None catch bass all day, every day, in all seasons. A secondary component in developing this new generation of bass flies must be situational appropriateness.

Another important component must be correct size. One principle well understood by the bait-casting community is that the larger bass we all pursue hit large baits much more readily than small ones. Simply put, large bass don't feed with the frequency of their yearling counterparts. A big bass might only feed once every 3 to 5 days. A small bass, on the other hand, feeds continuously. While the yearling consumes massive quantities of miniature prey, a lunker lies inert for lengthy periods in preparation to ambush a substantial meal. Small bass chase their prey. Larger ones ambush theirs. The size of the flies we throw becomes the next piece in the puzzle of future bass flies. Tomorrow's bass flies must be large enough to warrant a bass's attention, designed to create the action that triggers its predator instinct, and made for fishing in various locational situations.

Bass Senses and Behavior

An ichthyologist's understanding of taxonomy and bass behavior isn't really necessary to catch fish consistently, but we do need to know what makes ol' bucketmouth tick. There are several species and subspecies of the Centrarchidae family that could qualify for inclusion as largemouth bass. The Guadalupe Bass *(Micropterus treculi)* and Suwanee Bass *(Micropterus notius)* are two examples. Both are confined to a narrow range and neither commonly exceeds 10 to 12 inches in length. The focus of most largemouth bass fishing is the northern species *(Micropterus salmoides salmoides)* and the southern or Florida large-mouth *(Micropterus salmoides floridanus)*. Physical differences between the two, such as the number of scales along the fishes' lateral lines, were first noted by fisheries biologists in 1949. Later research indicated further differences including timing of the spawn, temperature tolerances and growth potential.

Still, genetic difference isn't a complete explanation for growth rates. Environment is a major factor. One published study titled "Effect of Air Temperature on Growth of Largemouth Bass in North America" concludes warm temperatures for extended periods of time is the most important factor in fish growth.

We also need to know a largemouth bass is a cold-blooded ambush predator with an immovable iris in its eye capable of color vision, nostrils with which to smell, and both an inner ear and lateral line used in hearing. It possesses a gaping mouth capable of taste and evaluating texture, and a relatively short, compact body built for short bursts of speed. Even its fins are able to evaluate by touch and detect odors.

Generally, a largemouth bass is most comfortable between 65 and 75 degrees. It seeks the comfort of that range or its metabolism slows noticeably as the water cools from 65 degrees, or hyperactivate above 75 degrees until sustained temperatures over 90 degrees become debilitating.

As ambush predators, largemouths seek the edges of cover fishermen have come to call structure where they can remain concealed from unsuspecting prey until they burst forth to complete the capture. Just as a lioness is able to isolate the one crippled or sickly gazelle from a herd of hundreds, so, too, can this freshwater predator focus undivided attention on the most vulnerable minnow in the school.

The iris of the human eye is capable of rapidly opening to allow more light inside and constricting to prevent it. Bass eyes can't do that, but they have the means of adjusting to bright light. The process is slow, however, which means they seek areas of relative darkness in which to lie. In shallow water this means shade. If there is none, they must go to deep water. The depth necessary to produce comfort for a bass eye depends on the amount of sunlight available, the water's clarity, and whether the light enters calm water directly or is refracted by choppy water.

While bass might not see color the same way humans do, there's little doubt some colors are more or less visible depending on light penetration and other factors. In a practical sense, we need to continually adjust our fly color selection and let success tell us what's preferred. There aren't any hard and fast rules regarding color selection, but experience has persuaded us to use brighter, light-reflecting colors when more light is available and darker colors capable of producing strong silhouettes when cloud cover, low sun angles, or darkness prevail.

There can be little doubt bass have the ability to smell or taste. Yet in tests we made in preparing for an article about commercially available scents, we never observed an instance in which largemouth bass moved toward scent independently of any other trigger. It seems logical that as ambush predators, bass are sight-and-sound oriented. We don't mean to imply foreign scents such as gasoline, tobacco, or even human odors don't serve as deterrents or manufactured scents are incapable of causing bass to hold onto the fly longer. In fact, many guides and bass experts use them regularly. We carry liquid soap with us to wash our hands after handling gasoline, outboard oil, insect repellant, and sunscreen.

On slowly-fished flies, it's our opinion texture also plays a role in whether a bass is inclined to hold or quickly reject a foreign object. If the fish is inclined to chase a rapidly retrieved fly, texture isn't important. Bass react with lightning speed to intercept fleeing prey and the hook will be set before the fly's expulsion occurs.

Lots of experts have said bass's keen sight is their most important sense when feeding. We disagree. Massive vegetation, lots of other underwater structure, as well as murky or unlit water make that almost impossible. Based on our many years of observation, we have come to believe bass often hear their prey first. Scientists confirm a bass's hearing is acute. These professionals theorize a bass can hear a motorboat a mile away. It makes sense then, that a bass has no difficulty "hearing" its prey or a fly entering the water. Its inner ear picks up those sounds and any others caused by movement in their environment. Further, we think the lateral line of the largemouth bass performs on the same function as our sonar locator units. That highly developed sensory organ enables the fish to precisely locate the position, size, shape, and even the density of the prey or fly long before it's seen. All this information stimulates its instincts to determine if the object's heft is worth the energy expenditure required in its capture.

While the home waters of virtually all other game fish are shrinking due to habitat degradation or remain static because no more can be created, largemouth bass waters continue to increase every day. New lakes and ponds are constantly added to the landscape. Clearly, the future of freshwater fly-fishing involves bass. Using larger rods and heavier leaders to manipulate big flies that incorporate lots of movement allows anglers a fighting chance with this brawling adversary.

Chapter 2

Understanding Bass Habitat

Understanding where largemouth bass can be located at any given time is the one truly critical piece of the bass-fishing puzzle. We can select all the right equipment, choose the perfect fly, manipulate it with consummate skill, but still fail to catch bass. If there aren't any fish present, we're just conducting casting practice. Under optimum conditions, more than 90 percent of any lake, pond or river is devoid of bass. Clearly we must understand the structural elements bass call home.

First, let's understand that any of these bass-holding structures can occur in different types of water. There are three possibilities: natural lakes, impoundments and moving waterways. We tend to classify each by size. Smaller still waters are ponds and larger ones are lakes, but those are arbitrary definitions at best. Whether a 36-acre body of still water is a small lake or a large pond is pretty much in the eye of the beholder. Moving water can be classified by size also. Larger moving waters are rivers while smaller ones are creeks. That's obvious, but moving water has other classifications we must address. A bayou, by definition, is a sluggish body of water that flows through a marshy area and connects two other bodies of water. Brackish water, where salt and fresh water meet, is affected by tides. These areas are homes to largemouth bass, too.

Much has been made, and volumes written, about the disparities in each of these waters from the bass fisherman's perspective, but it's not necessary for a fly-caster to learn how to fish all over again just because the body of water is different. A pond fisherman shouldn't be bewildered just because he's fishing a lake, because the elements of structure are the same. The only difference is the size of the water. A natural lake shouldn't confuse an impoundment fly-fisher; the only difference in switching from still water to moving water is the adjustment to current.

Nearly all types of structures are available in all bodies of water. If we learn how to present flies to all the kinds of structure we are apt to encounter and how to adapt to current, we can fish for bass virtually anywhere.

Largemouth bass are dependent upon structure. In fact, most bass are related to it most of the time. The only exception occurs when bass suspend.

In terms of bass fishing, we define structure as any irregular feature that's different from its surrounding area. It can be a little stump in a foot of water that disrupts a silt-covered shoreline or it could be an old creek bed in 20 feet of water that meanders through a lake cove. It could be a boat dock attached to shore or a submerged hump in the middle of the lake. To be of value to the resident bass population, it must have close access to relatively deep water. Deeper water offers bass an escape from danger. Without deep water nearby, large bass won't use shallow structure.

Looking for the exception identifies the best part of the structure. Find the largest hump or the lowest indentation in an area where the bottom is irregular. Seek the largest stump with the most branches. Target the largest bunch of weeds in the bed. Big bass are most often related to the best structure.

Not all bodies of water have all of the following examples of structure. Many waters have very few of them, but it's possible for some waters to be so diverse they have nearly all. Let's take a look at the most common types of structure and explain why each can be attractive to largemouth bass.

Dams and Spillways

A dam, of course, is indigenous only to impounded waters. It can be constructed of a variety of materials, and this, in part, can determine the area's suitability for bass. Most of the time the dam hosts the impoundment's deepest water. Dams can be constructed of concrete, earth or earth with riprap facing. Each composition can provide ambush points for bass, but often the best is riprap facing because its many crevices harbor crayfish and other bass prey. Bass frequent riprap and forage along the face of it. Look for irregularities such as protrusions formed by piles of rocks or indentations in the rock wall. Depending on its location and size, it can be home to several big bass. Corners of the dam where it's flanked by adjoining banks can also harbor some fish. Another prime location is riprap in combination with any other piece of structure. A washed-in deadfall for example, along an otherwise unbroken line of riprap, could hold the key to the dam's resident population. Similarly, there can be a patch of weeds somewhere along the dam's face that attracts baitfish and bass.

Mechanical spillways are structures that allow water to overflow from the reservoir when the lake is full and more water enters the basin. There are dozens of different kinds, but they all offer unique and often over-looked fishing opportunities. When the spillway is flowing it draws potential food sources to it, and as a result, bass line up facing away from the spillway to allow their meals to wash to them. In older, heavily silted waters there is often a pile of silt and debris surrounding the spillway that washed into the area in times of heavy rains. These piles provide prime structural habitat even when the spillway isn't active.

Inlet Creeks

Anyplace a moving body of water enters still water can attract bass. Moving water can bring warmer water into a cool lake or cool water into a warm one. In rivers, warmer water in spring and fall and cooler water in summer can flow in from tributaries. Delivery of warmer water from creeks sometimes happens in early spring when a lake or pond is still too cool for much bass activity. If the inflow warms the immediate area even a degree or two, it can prompt bass to move toward it. Inflow can come from a small nearby spring that warms cold water and, conversely, cools warm water. Both are a great advantage to the bass population, but the benefit of inlet creeks doesn't end there. They also wash in food and introduce oxygenated water to a stagnant environment.

Years ago we lived near a backwater oxbow lake. Years of siltation had removed most of the mid-lake structure so it resembled a fish bowl. What was visible above the water was pretty much the extent of available cover. A small spring ran through a culvert under the lakeshore's road and emerged in some willows that lined either side of the spring's path into the lake. The area was a bass magnet. In the summertime, we frequently went there armed with streamers and caught bass up to 19 inches. Stained water hid us from the fish even on cloudless days, and tiny spinners added to our flies' hook bends enhanced their attractiveness.

An inlet creek can also enter moving water and create large, slow eddies and pockets of still water at the edges of the confluence. If appropriate depth and cover accompany the tributary's mouth, it can be an important feeding location for largemouths.

Wash Areas After Rains

A wash area is a little draw that's dry except when it funnels runoff into a body of water. After an early spring rain, water in the immediate area that receives the runoff can become slightly warmer and provide the critical difference in temperature that can attract bass. At other times, the wash area can bring oxygenated water and food into the system for opportunistic largemouths. If other cover and deep water is present, it can be a situational hotspot.

We used to launch a car-top boat on a small city water supply lake that had six wash areas. Two entered the backs of tiny coves that were too shallow to hold fish, but the others entered the little lake at the base of a bluff made by the old creek channel. Two entered at the bluff's ends, and the remaining two had carved notches through its top and charged steeply down its face. We've endured many rainy fishing trips waiting for enough water to activate those washes. Once, a guest took a 22-inch bass from one of them on just such an occasion. When he returned during drier weather he always insisted on making a few casts there despite any explanation we could offer.

Bottom Composition Changes

Any bottom area where the composition changes can attract bass. If there is no other structure nearby there probably won't be a resident population, but any of these seam areas can draw foraging fish. Areas that abruptly change from sand to gravel or from rock to mud are likely candidates to attract bass because they can offer two or more different prey choices. For example, a gravel bar, which attracts minnows feeding on microorganisms, can attach to a shoreline of chunk rock where crayfish are abundant. If there are weeds, stumps, or deadfalls nearby there's no reason for the bass to wander. All of their needs are met in one relatively small area.

Even in miniature waters, these areas of change can be important. One pond we occasionally fished was heavily silted, but there were clumps of bankside willows growing intermittently along its shore. We discovered quite by accident while wading that the bottom was substantially firmer near the willows than on either side of them. In this particular pond, areas of firm bottom were preferred as spawning sites, but the softer-bottomed shoreline was ignored.

Bottom composition changes are particularly significant when locating bass in rivers. Look for them in areas with the least amount of current, which are preferred by largemouth bass. Willows, rootwads, and bulrushes, for example, can signal a change in bottom composition in addition to providing cover and prey.

Points

A point is land attached to shore at one end that extends into increasingly deeper water. Like the rest of the surrounding bottom, its content could be almost anything and can be diverse within itself. It can be barren or covered by stumps, deadfalls, rocks, or weeds. Points can occur on little ponds or sprawling lakes. Ignore the ones without cover.

Points can be an excellent place to begin a fishing trip. There's water from quite shallow to deep and every depth in between. Points with good

Diagram 2-A

cover are capable of hosting large populations of big fish year around. Often one side of the point is superior to the other. Usually this is due to the accessibility of deep water, but it can also involve the type of cover present and its relation to sunlight penetration.

We're familiar with one little pond that has a point so small it's possible to roll cast along its entire length. One side becomes a shallow flat that extends into a small cove. The other side drops away into the main basin of the pond. The submerged ridge of the point is covered with coontail. By positioning a float tube off the end of the point, flies can be cast into the shallows and retrieved along the edge of the weedline at various depths. The times when at least one largemouth can't be caught along that little point are rare.

Another of our favorite points is located on a nearby reservoir. It juts into the water for more than a hundred yards and is stair-stepped along one side. It's located along a main submerged river channel and likely has an almost imperceptible current flowing along one side. The area receives lots of pleasure boat and jet ski traffic, but mid-week trips there can produce some good catches by dropping heavily weighted flies from one level to the next (Diagram 2-A).

Islands

Islands are, for the fisherman's purpose, closely related to points. They rise out of the depths to provide shallow to relatively deep water all in one package, and they often connect to the nearest shore with an underwater ridge. Again, the key is additional structure. Weeds, rocks, or deadfalls can enhance the structure's attractiveness. Lots of anglers simply fish their way around the island, but it's far better to determine the best points and fish them thoroughly. Like the riprap dam discussed earlier, it's subtle changes in the composition of an island that are important. An inlet, a projection, a pile of rocks or an old duck blind can provide the point that attracts bass. If the island is connected to the nearest land by an underwater ridge, it's worth checking. The steepest side of the ridge sloping into the lake's depths is the most likely bass-holding structure.

River islands provide many current breaks where water eddies slowly or becomes slack. The head and tail of the island provide two common areas largemouths occupy while they wait for food to come to them. The side of the island where the current is slower can collect logs, brush, and other structure, and the resultant pockets become ambush locations for bass.

Humps and Depressions

Humps are closely related to both islands and points. They're areas that seem to rise from deep water toward the surface a few inches or many feet, but don't quite make it. "Wannabe" islands.

One such hump far out in a northern lake comes to mind. Its closest encounter with the surface was at 3 feet and bulrushes grew on its crown. When their tops emerged from the water, they drew some fishing pressure. Before then, a fly could be stripped through the tops of the rushes without interference. When other fishermen discovered the weed-covered hump top, it was time to bounce heavily weighted flies down the rocky slope of its steepest side. The hump once surrendered a 21-inch bass to a fishing companion. When we returned to the lodge our friend was anxious to tell about the big fish we'd insisted he release. He blurted out the news about the mid-lake hump, and everyone within hearing distance knew exactly where we'd been. No doubt the top of the ridge got lots of attention in succeeding days, but it's a good bet that lunker's home on the rocky ledge was never invaded.

Roadways submerged when large reservoirs were formed are humps, although their configurations are less obvious. Bass relate to the roads' shoulders, and accompanying fence rows, road signs, brush, and windrows also provide structure. The shallower portions can be easily identified without locators if they are used as unimproved lake accesses. Observing the size and age of trees on shore can indicate other submerged roads. If there's a swath of small trees and brush leading to the shoreline amid older, taller trees, for example, there might have been a road there at one time whose bed and shoulders could still be intact. Identifying these old roads requires a locator.

Discovering depressions in the lake bottom can be equally valuable. We believe depressions are used primarily as staging areas and as retreats when post cold-front conditions drive bass from their regular routine.

Creek Channels

Creek channels can run from the backs of coves into the main lake where they join another, larger riverbed. They're like a system of highways that traverse most reservoirs. Generally, those that run through the main body of a large lake are simply too deep to be of any value, either to the bass or those who chase them. When they're found in more than 20 feet of water, they're just not viable, but those that enter from secondary coves to join another channel from an adjacent cove can be important to understanding fish movement within that area. Once again, it's important to look for unusual features. First, search for attending structure. Submerged brushy banks, submerged bridges or old culverts can help you locate bass. Next, look for U-bends, S-bends (Diagram 2-B, page 36), saddles (Diagram 2-B), and creek junctions. If a larger stream enters one of the secondary coves, look for its submerged inside bends where there could have been shoals. The key to submerged creek channels is depth. Our rule of thumb is if any of the structural properties just described exists in less than 20 feet of water, we'll give it a try. If this area is at all open, with humps or rock piles, some fish should be seen on the locator. Don't try to cast to individual fish, but instead, concentrate your efforts where the most fish activity is found.

Bluffs

Bluffs occur where the land seems to end abruptly, then drops sharply into the water. These steep banks can be composed of hard rocks, soft flaky shale, clay or dirt and present themselves as high cliffs or tall mud embankments. Whether bass use the bluff or not depends on what's at its base. There can be piles of rocks or other materials that have eroded from the bluff or an old creek channel that once swept along its base. There can be stumps, humps, brush or any variety of other structure associated with the old creek channel. The bluff itself isn't as significant as the irregularities associated with it. If an old creek channel bends to meet the bluff, the two areas between the channel and the submerged bluff upstream and downstream from the bend form shelves. These shelves can be the bluff's most productive parts (Diagram 2-C). Shelves created over eons usually offer protected ambush points and accessible deep water. Some shelves are terraced with different levels. These areas can be used

Diagram 2-B

by largemouths as staging areas or places they use while in transition from the deeper main lake to shallower coves, especially if there are vegetation, woodpiles, or rocks that clutter the shelf. They can also be places where bass spend an entire summer season.

We fish a long, rock bluff that has a transitional shelf on one side and a summer home for bass on the other. The transitional shelf is a great

Diagram 2-C

location in the early pre-spawn when water temperatures are in the low fifties, and is again productive in the fall as bass move to deep water at the base of the bluff. The summer shelf is largely overlooked by lots of fishermen because the inundated creek channel traverses the main lake to join the bluff. This shelf is quite large, covered in old brush, and is in close proximity to a small gravel and clay-bottomed cove suitable for spawning. Three of the last four years, our largest bass of the season has come from this area. Bluff walls can have many projections and indentations capable of holding bass. All should be checked thoroughly, as should any area where a creek channel separates slightly from a bluff.

Many anglers fish a bluff by drifting or trolling along its face within easy casting distance of the water's edge. If the bluff is terraced it's a good plan, but there's another option that might work better. Try positioning your boat so casts can be made in either direction along the base of the bluff. When wind or waves push you too close, readjust your position. This is an area where sinking lines are used almost exclusively.

Fish shallow structures when the bluff draws full shade. If the bluff is located on an east shore, we would call it a morning bluff, whereas west shore bluffs are evening bluffs. Deeper areas can be fished effectively even when the sun is high and intense.

Undercut Banks

Wave action on still water or current in moving water erode the shore at the waterline, and the result is sometimes an undercut bank that provides cool, overhead cover for summer bass. In natural lakes, the undercut bank can be composed of rock that water has worn away over time. In impounded waters, undercut banks can occur when a layer of soft rock is exposed and crumbles away. If the catalyst is an inlet creek, the hollowed out bank is a perfect lair for an ambush predator. Undercuts in clay exposed to sun and wave action are not good targets, but protected ones near deep water can be prime locations.

Retaining Walls

Manmade walls constructed along the shoreline for cosmetics or to prevent erosion can attract bass if there's attending structure and the walls' locations are advantageous to bass. Retaining walls that are always sunlit with no cover won't attract fish. Look for vegetation growing along the walls' faces or at their corners, or the presence of wood in the form of stumps, logs, deadfall, or attached docks and walkways. If walls also have morning or evening shade they can be worth investigating. If they're composed of irregular rock or concrete and receive lots of shade, they can be homes to bass forage. Look for corners, places between the walls and their attending structures, where bass can safely locate while watching for prey. Usually, the focus for bass anglers is other structure rather than the walls themselves.

Wood Structure

Wood structure can be the natural variety, such as stumps, rootwads, standing timber, logjams, or brush or man-made, such as docks, attending walkways, or duck blinds. Both types of structure provide excellent cover for largemouth bass. Overhead protection, shade, and attached algae growth that harbor bass prey are among the leading attractions. Selecting the best wood structure can be difficult on water where it's abundant, such as coves full of standing timber.

Docks provide excellent largemouth habitat, but not all docks are created equal. The best are those near deep water and natural cover.

Standing timber on a point near a creek channel or a large logjam pounded into the shore by prevailing winds can be good locations. To attract bass, standing timber and logjams must offer access to relatively deep water and be located in water of appropriate depth. In murky, weedy, or shady coves, appropriate can mean shallow. It could be as deep as 20 feet in clear water if there's sunlight penetration.

In the right situation, standing timber can be fished similarly to stumps, but when it's located in deep water bass locate in the upper limbs. This can be a late-autumn or wintering pattern, and a large population of bass, generally in the same year class, suspend among branches. Usually, weather determines where bass locate at any given time. On sunny days, we've found largemouths scattered along the outer branches of large trees covered by only 4 feet of water over a 35-foot

39

bottom. We concluded the sun warmed the water's upper layer by a degree or two and the bass were seeking warmth. They're more active in warmer water temperatures, and, consequently, more likely to feed. When we find bass close to tree trunks, they're usually not inclined to feed. Bass are opportunistic and might grab flies that swim past their noses, but when they're related to the interiors of trees, chasing flies is out of the question.

A miniature bass factory can have but one deadfall that extends from shore into deep water. It could be assumed bass hold somewhere along the deadfall's length virtually all the time. The problem with isolated structures in small waters is while you know where much of the bass population is located, so does the rest of the world. The fly-fisher has a great advantage in this situation because the fish are accustomed to heavy splashdowns from large spinners or plastic worms. A fly could be something they've never seen. Take care not to cast shadows on the water and don't bump into tree trunks or their branches. Noise and vibrations send warnings to every fish along the entire deadfall. If the deadfall is approached from the water side, make your initial casts to the deepest branches farthest from the tree's main trunk, then work progressively shallower to avoid spooking the bass.

Stumps should be fished carefully from many different angles. First consideration should be given to the shady side of shallow stumps. While you're there, cast to the stump's sunlit side near its misshapen projections or indentations that can serve to shield bass from penetrating light. Hard-headed jigs and similar patterns are good choices, and intentionally pulling your fly into the stump, then pulling it away can be an effective tactic.

Multiple projections that provide cover and shade make rootwads potential bass magnets. In moving waters, they are significant current blockers. In an area where the bottom is soft, current dishes out a hole on the downstream side that's an excellent bass hangout. The fish are out of the current and a constant food supply sweeps past their position.

Logjams, including abandoned beaver houses, can harbor large bass populations, but their irregular features can also be real fly grabbers. To be successful, the fly must actually enter the chaos of jutting branches

Diagram 2-D

and crisscrossed trunks, so weed guards are a must. Sinking lines must be kept under direct control before they sink into harm's way. Cutting an expensive full-sinking line free of its snag is a sad experience. Scout these areas thoroughly with a locator, if possible, then count down the offering into the fish zone before attempting to maneuver the fly. When the fish hits, it's important the rod and tippet are stout enough to wrench the bass away from tough cover.

Boat docks can be attractive to bass because they offer lots of overhead cover and shade, but not all docks are created equal. If the boat dock is attached to shore and its outer edges extend over deeper water with immediate access to protective depths, it's good bass-holding structure. If other kinds of cover are present, such as weeds, brush or sunken Christmas trees, the dock could be an exceptional location (Diagram 2-D).

One additional feature that accompanies some docks is a fish-cleaning station. If the dock owner uses it regularly, it's a good bet the area's biggest largemouths hang around for feeding time. We might assume it would take the fish a long time to discover such hand outs, but it doesn't. Our experience is in less than 24 hours bass and other game fish are drawn to the drain. Just as with bird feeders, there's a pecking order; the larger fish eat first.

Duck blinds are another manmade structure bass seem to love. Blinds provide overhead cover and shade, but the same requirements for depth and additional cover apply.

Years ago, we fished a 35-acre lake that had a decrepit old duck blind that stood in 6 feet of water and was connected to shore by a plank walkway. After many seasons of non-use, beavers decimated its supporting posts on one side. Their activity had lowered one end of the shooter's box so it hung into the water rather than above it. As the front of the blind rotted and fell away, it exposed one side of the partially submerged box. We often caught bass from the shaded area under the old blind, including one 18-incher, but we also caught several bass from the submerged part of the blind. It was a two-story apartment house for bass. The ravages of time eventually brought the old duck blind down, and the only thing left the last time we were there was a post. The bass, of course, had relocated.

Other manmade wooden structures can provide important cover. Swimming platforms, boathouses, and goose nests can provide cover for bass. We've even caught bass in the Illinois River from the shaded side of temporarily moored barges. They hardly qualify as wooden structures, but the principle is the same.

Submerged Fence Rows

Fences that continue into the water, and those that accompany former roadways hold windblown wood or brush that grew there before the water was impounded. Over time, fence posts and wires become trellises for algae growth and stringy moss, and minnows and fry hide in the underwater curtain. Shallow ends near shore often provide lots of inviting pockets.

Vegetation

There are so many varieties of aquatic plants that listing them here is impossible. Fortunately, a botanist's understanding isn't required to grasp how vegetation impacts the lives of bass. By vegetation, we mean plants that grow in the water. We refer to some of the more common varieties here simply as examples.

In some waters, vegetation is lush and nearly too abundant. Despite its obvious advantages of providing a sun block, cooling the water, aiding the oxygenation process, and attracting prey species, plants are sometimes frustrating. Hooks fouled with stringy moss or caught on plant leaves and stems with virtually every cast make productive fishing difficult. Even weedless hooks aren't much help. The rich environment, however, is beneficial to bass. In addition to comfort and food, it provides a rearing area for fry and numerous ambush points for adults.

In heavily weeded waters, no single area easily stands out as a locational factor. Just as a mile of riprap won't always hold fish all along its entire length, so, too, is the case with vegetation. In each instance, it's the exception that's important. If we're fishing along a straight shoreline with coontail extending to the surface from a depth of 12 feet, we fish the points and pockets in the weedline. By targeting the unusual features and casting to them from various angles using a variety of presentations, we maximize opportunities for positive hookups. Diversity is important; look for the places one kind of vegetation meets another. We should be on the lookout for other kinds of structure in connection with vegetation. A row of stumps, a deadfall, or a pile of rocks can take on much greater importance amid this aquatic jungle. A deadfall could get little use by the bass population if it's part of a long series of similar woodpiles, but a deadfall with vegetation can be a bass magnet. If the water we're fishing has little vegetation, a small patch of weeds could draw many feeding bass. Finding differences, then, is the key to finding bass lairs.

Because one aquatic plant can be very different from another, it might be necessary to present flies much differently. Depending on sunlight penetration and other factors, milfoil can grow 20 feet to the water's surface where its tips bend to lie flat. Bulrushes, on the other hand, have tough, more rigid stems and grow a few feet above the surface. In each case, the bass hunter is looking for pockets, points or holes in and along the weedline, but fishing the irregularities of each kind of vegetation requires a different approach. Milfoil's fragile stems enable the angler to deposit the fly in a pocket where branches are quite sparse. When the inevitable weed contact is made, a firm strip frees the fly, which can often continue its journey toward the rod tip. The commotion caused by the fly's contact with the weed stem can provoke a lethargic bass into investigating, but in a similarly sparse pocket of bulrushes a hung fly is likely to remain attached to a much firmer stem. Offering the same fly equipped with a weed guard can solve the problem, but switching to a bendback version or a surface fly could be necessary.

The problem of fishing in a "salad" without hanging up is no less severe when fishing the surface. Chugging a popper over the tops of soft coontail isn't nearly as difficult as negotiating a patch of lily pads.

Floating vegetation, such as water hyacinth, offers cool, overhead cover and shade for bass. Baitfish and fry hide underneath while leaves and stems above water are insect habitat. Growth of floating vegetation usually begins at the shoreline, but might or might not extend over deep water because wind pushes the colonies into many different locations. Inside pockets and outer edges of the rafts are primary fishing targets.

Brush

Brush growing above the surface should also be considered structure. Shrubs, such as multiflora rose and buttonbush, often grow on the shoreline or banks above it. Brush can be partially submerged or grow with its roots on dry land and its branches hanging over the water's surface. Such shrubs support insects, birds, reptiles, amphibians, and mammals within their many branches, and the food and shade they offer fish below makes them significant to the bass fisherman.

Mapping Structure

Becoming intimately familiar with bass-holding structure in the water you fish isn't easy. It involves understanding the length, width, shape, and depth of something largely unseen. Good topographical maps and locators are helpful, of course, but they don't provide all the answers. We might see a brush pile on a map, then locate it on a graph unit, but, as we sit in our boats, we might still wonder exactly where the drop-off begins and precisely where the top of the brush reaches. Numerous casts and subsequent hang-ups are required to become comfortable with fishing

Standing timber is prime habitat for many reservoir largemouths.

there. It's one of the reasons we all tend to be more successful on waters we fish regularly.

Visualization is very helpful in gaining a complete understanding of underwater structure. As we're driving, we imagine the landscape as a lake bottom and make mental notes of the places bass would be located with the sun at the particular angle at the time of day, the wind from the present direction, and the comparable season and temperatures. Sure, it's just a mental exercise, but it helps us understand the elements of structure.

Exceptions

Largemouth bass rely upon structure nearly all the time, but there are a couple of notable exceptions.

One is when extremely bad weather occurs in the summer. Bass scattered along a shoreline weedbed, for example, often simply back off the structure and suspend over deep water. Our observation is they remain in this suspended state, very tightly bunched, until the weather changes and stabilizes. The situation has no value to the angler during the intense part of the storm, but it helps explain the bass's whereabouts afterward.

The other significant period when bass suspend occurs in mid- to late summer or early autumn in impoundments where shad are a major portion of the bass's diet. At this time, schools of gizzard or threadfin shad cruise the lake's upper layer feeding on microorganisms suspended in the surface film. This activity seems to occur with greater frequency within large coves as thousands of shad cruise about. Bass frequently slash through shad schools, which causes them to spray into the air in a frantic attempt to escape the attack. This event is called a "shad burst," and it can provide some wild fishing action. Our experience with shad bursts is bass pursuing a particular school all belong to the same year class. Usually, these suspended and pursuing bass are 12 to 15 inches. While this can provide some great action, it's not unheard of for larger bass to participate in this activity. Far more commonly, larger bass cruise several feet below the schools to grab wounded and unconsumed shad that flutter to them vertically after smaller bass's savage attacks on the surface. Since movements of these schools of shad schools are erratic, it can be difficult to follow them. Although it's best accomplished with a powerful trolling motor, shad are easily spooked and care must be taken not to approach them too closely or to cast directly into the school.

An excellent fly for fishing shad bursts is the Squirrel Spin. The pattern, given in Chapter 5, has a small spinner attached to the hook bend and wings of stacked gray squirrel tail. Clousers, staples in bass fly-fishers' boxes, are an obvious choice. Bass are infuriatingly size-selective when it comes to shad bursts and reject everything that's either too small or too large, so the size of the fly must match the size of the shad perfectly for the time of year.

During the period when shad activity occurs, we often abandon the search for larger fish to cruise the mouths of coves looking for eruptions that indicate shad bursts. Hundreds of bursts covering many acres can occur in the same cove. It's just too much fun to pass up.

Rising water presents another exceptional situation in structure-based bass fishing. There are several instances in which rising water provides a smorgasbord for bass.

A quick, hard rain can run off very quickly causing a pond to rise, and, in the process, engulf grasshoppers, mice, worms, and other edibles. A rising river can flow into an oxbow lake where largemouths congregate near the floodwaters' entry points to feed and take advantage of freshly oxygenated water. Rising waters tend to be muddy and can carry lots of debris, so fishing soon after the rise can be frustrating. Dark flies and slow retrieves are most successful when fishing murky water.

Yet another instance of rising water occurs daily in coastal rivers where saltwater mixes with freshwater. Brackish water creates a unique fishery and fishing rising tides can be the key to finding good action. Often grass beds and islands provide current breaks that can be good locations. Floater/divers, dragonfly imitations, and mid-depth minnow imitations are good fly choices for brackish bass that seem invigorated by the salt and are often exceptional fighters.

Fishing structure is fundamental to bass fishing. The better acquainted you become with the structure available in the waters you fish, the better you will get to know the largemouth population.

Chapter 3

Approach, Delivery, and Fly Animation

It's easy to understand why many fly-fishers regard casting prowess as the solution to all their fish-catching problems. Few other acts among sportsmen are alone so satisfying. Fly-rodders can become so preoccupied with the almost hypnotic rhythm of the cast all of the other elements required to entice the fish are neglected. Fishing must be viewed as a whole concept that consists of the angler's approach to the fish, the delivery of the fly and its animation. Performing one of these functions successfully without regard to the others is simply an exercise in futility, and precious few bass are fooled.

Successful largemouth fly-fishers are focused on hooking and fighting the next bass. Equipment is merely a tool, and physical skills a means to the same end. Once, at a large fly-fishing exposition we watched one of fly-fishing's most recognizable personalities as he spoke to a sizeable audience. He had a rack with 20 fly rods on stage with him, and as he gesticulated the rods were bumped and fell to the floor in a heap. Onlookers gasped as several thousand dollars worth of exquisite long rods tumbled to the floor. Almost oblivious to the mishap, the speaker simply stepped across the pile and continued with his thought. To him the rods were simply tools, while the audience gave them a much higher importance. The point isn't that fine rods should not be valued, enjoyed, and well cared for, but simply that they exist first and foremost to perform a practical function.

The fisherman's approach to the bass-fishing situation includes bank stalking and any of a variety of methods that place the angler near, in or on the water.

Bank Stalking

The most frequently applied approach is bank stalking. And why not? There are millions of small ponds and stock tanks scattered across the United States, and a high percentage of them have resident populations of largemouth bass. In ponds, bass fly-rodding is reduced to its most basic form, and fishing along the shores of these small waters can be as productive as any other method. There's no extra equipment to purchase or manage and there's no watercraft to maneuver. All that's necessary are the rod, reel, line, leader, and a box of flies.

To enhance their efforts, anglers should first be aware of the way they approach the water. Some come to the water's edge noisily with brightly colored clothing and reflective watches and sunglasses. They wouldn't consider hunting deer or turkey in the same way, but they fail to recognize the similarities of the activities. The well-camouflaged bass has a much better chance of seeing the angler than vice versa, and its watery environment conducts sound so efficiently any excessive vibration or noise is immediately transmitted through its lateral line. The distances at which largemouths are capable of detecting noisy approaches are remarkable. It would not be an exaggeration to say the bass population of an entire pond could be put on red alert by a single loud approach. We're reminded of the time we observed a pair of fishermen carry a car-top boat into a pond and nearly throw the craft into the water. They hurriedly cast to the edges with little action before disgustedly pulling their boat out and heading for another pond "where they're hitting." After resting the water for 20 or 30 minutes and making a careful and quiet approach, the action miraculously improved.

Bank-bound anglers in particular should approach their sport with the preparations and attitudes of good hunters. Stalking is just the right choice of words to describe the process. Clothing that blends into the background is necessary, and camouflage apparel isn't overkill. Plan your fly selections and methods beforehand. Sneak softly and slowly into position before casting and crouch or kneel where necessary. Even in muddy waters, sudden shadows can startle fish. It's true you can agitate a bass into striking by repeated casts to the same lair, but the bigger fish are very wary of sloppy presentations, a hang-up, or ripping the flyline from the water. It just doesn't make sense to defeat your own chances for success with thoughtless approaches and bad preparations.

With few exceptions, every small fishing environment offers only a limited selection of places where casts can or should be made. From each of those positions, however, there's any number of different casting targets. Refer to Diagram 3-A as we discuss examples.

Let's assume this typical impounded pond is small enough to allow the angler to fish completely around its shoreline. One common mistake is simply walking all along the bank casting ahead of you. You might well stumble into some of the more productive areas, but far too much time is spent casting to water that's devoid of fish. Knowing the types of structure preferred by bass for a given set of weather and seasonal conditions enables us to go directly to those points and concentrate on our delivery and retrieve.

Choosing an arbitrary starting point at the left-hand corner of the riprap dam allows us to carefully approach the dam region and fan-cast along the riprap and across the shallow corner to the weedline. After each casting session, pull back and take a route well away from shore to the next casting location to avoid spooking fish. On any given trip, depending upon season and weather conditions, we might skip some of the possible casting positions.

Position Number 2, for example, is a good location when bass are shallow, but a very poor stop when they're almost certainly deep, as they are in late fall. In each location, the entire area of any fish-holding structure should be thoroughly fan-cast. Several, or even repeated, casts to the most likely spots are prudent. It might even be a good idea to change flies or color patterns, then begin again.

When cloud cover prevents much sunlight penetration, largemouth bass are shallow if adequate food and cover are present. Under those

Diagram 3-A

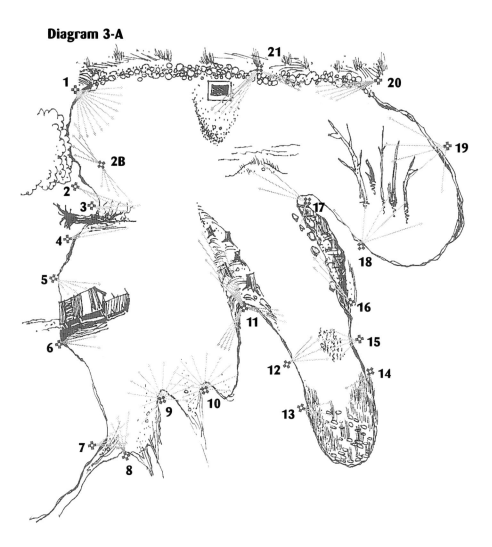

conditions, positions Number 2, 2b, 3, 4, 5, 6, 11, 12, 13, 14, and 15 deserve the attention. On a warm, cloudless summer morning, on the other hand, it's more productive to cast to the deepest parts of 3, 4, 5, 6, 11, 15, 16, 17, 18, 19, 20, and 21. In early spring when pond temperatures are still in the forties, fish positions 7 and 8 carefully. Right after a midsummer rain, concentrated efforts at 9 and 10 can find opportunistic bass feeding on life forms that have washed into the pond. Fish the muddy water's edge, too. Pulling a fly from the darkened waters into clear water or vice versa can trigger hits.

Wade Fishing

Wading offers the angler an opportunity to get into a more advantageous position or to avoid backcasts into brush or tall grasses. But there are some hazards to consider. First, and most obviously, some areas are simply too deep to accommodate wading. In ponds that have been subjected to siltation, the bottom is usually too soft to permit safe wading. A wading staff can help determine how deep you might sink into the muck, and the need for good judgment cannot be overstated.

Even if it's safe, the practice of entering the water, then wading around the pond is an especially bad idea. The disturbance of the bottom such activity can have on plant life, insect larva, crustaceans, and even on bass spawning beds is considerable. In addition, it's inconsiderate of any angler who might follow the muddy trail. Instead, pick points of entry carefully and fan-cast the area thoroughly before withdrawing to proceed to the next point of entry.

Position 2b has been included to show how a brushy bank with overhanging branches can cause the angler to be better served by wading. Notice the fisherman has the opportunity to turn around and cast under the shaded canopy of overhanging branches. On days when bright sun sends many of the bass into deeper water, the protected area and the dock at Positions 5 and 6 might provide the only shallow opportunities in the entire pond.

Another advantage afforded the wading angler is casts are made from a lower profile that's less visible to the bass. Positions 2b, 5, 6, 9, 10, 11, 12, 13, 14, and 15 might offer good wading opportunities.

Watercraft

While there are many exceptions, the size of the body of water you're fishing determines the type of craft used. Generally, smaller waters are best suited for personal watercraft. Car-top boats and canoes are more at home on mid-sized waters, while larger boats are usually restricted to big waters.

The major advantage to inflatables is portability. They can be conveniently and easily carried into waters where boat-launching is impossible. Inflatables are anything but new. According to Deke Meyer, author of two books on the subject, " . . . in his narrative about his 1843 expedition that explored the West, John C. Fremont wrote about using an 18-foot inflatable rubber boat." Meyer reports there were personal inflatables in use in Europe as early as 1911, and they became commercially available in the United States in 1947. Our own experiences with personal watercrafts date to the mid-sixties when we purchased a molded plastic model. It served our needs for many years before an irreparable leak forced it into retirement and more modern inflatables were purchased.

Today's personal watercraft covers are made from non-rotting nylon and have double air chambers for safety. They're comfortable and convenient; they can be used for fishing inaccessible places on large waters, packing into remote areas; they're perfect for exploring ponds and strip pits.

The original was a round tube that required the angler to step into the center and pull the tube around him. The angler was perched on a seat while his legs dangled beneath for propulsion and control. They're still around, and their major advantage is they're least expensive.

Modern float tubes are wedge-shaped, which provides superior stability. A small air compressor that plugs into a vehicle's cigarette lighter inflates them in a few minutes. It's a noisy apparatus, but it completes the job in the time it takes to put on waders and assemble rods.

The only additional equipment needed is a pair of fins or foot paddles. Fins allow backward propulsion with ease and relative speed. Foot paddles only enable forward movement with the backward thrust of a leg, which makes them rather inefficient if moving farther than 50 yards is required. Fins are obviously the best choice when the water is too large to be covered with foot paddles, but when we fish small ponds with lots of deadfalls and brush the paddles allow us to face our targets and maneuver with accuracy.

Another option is the open-bow float tube. It's designed so the angler can simply slide into the tube from the front. This is infinitely easier, and there are other advantages as well. Their open design and the materials used in their construction make them lighter to carry and faster on the water.

There are also personal watercraft models that are designed so anglers have the options of using fins or oars for propulsion. One such version is an open-bottomed inflatable raft. Another has two separate tubes attached like pontoons. The design of the latter causes far less resistance to the water and therefore is much easier and faster to fin or row.

The Coast Guard requires a life vest be worn while float tubing. It's also a good idea to float tube with a companion who could help in case of emergency.

Although we use our tubes most on small waters, we've occasionally taken them by boat to sheltered coves on large reservoirs for fishing snag-ridden backwaters inaccessible to other lake users. In spite of the blaze-orange patches designed to make the tubes more visible, their low profile excludes them from the view of faster crafts. Even if that wasn't a problem, being tossed about or flipped over in the wakes of speedboats and jet skis could make for a fatal day on the water.

Canoes offer the adventurous bass chaser reasonable portability, excellent maneuverability, and a low profile while allowing the caster to stay dry. Many also regard fly-fishing from canoes as a classic experience. They're easy to launch and enable anglers to reach bass waters wider, heavier boats can't. Canoes are ideal for waters that are too shallow for most motorized boats and make it possible to explore the mouths of inlet creeks on large reservoirs and tributaries of major rivers. They're the only reasonable solution for fishing flooded timber, brush, and undergrowth so dense there are only a few boat lanes. Canoes are hard to control in the wind, however, and usually one companion controls the craft while the other fishes.

Boats are manufactured in a nearly infinite number of styles from small aluminum prams to classically styled wooden crafts handmade by skilled artisans. Knowing what's best for the type of water available determines the style of boat best suited for those waters. Budget considerations are also a factor and the choices can range in price from a few hundred dollars to many thousands.

If the waters you want to reach are relatively small with either no boat-launching facility or one of the unimproved varieties, a small, inexpensive lightweight cartop model powered by oars or an electric trolling motor is the best choice. For those who regularly challenge large, windy, lakes with considerable boat traffic a little pram is just plain dangerous. A larger, heavier, more stable craft with enough horsepower to get off the water when an unexpected storm arrives make the most sense. If you fish shallow, grass- or weed-covered lakes, perhaps a canoe or an airboat is the only choice for quickly maneuvering through such waters without hanging up.

Bass boats, originally designed to meet the needs of tournament fishermen, are accommodating for fly-fishers as well. They provide stable casting platforms and great comfort, but there can be too many exposed knobs, handles, and cables to grab loose fly line. Select a boat for its fly-fisher friendliness in design and accessories.

The basics of positioning and control, however, are the same for all watercraft. Diagram 3-B shows the same body of water used to demonstrate bank fishing and wade casting positions in Diagram 3-A. In that example, we envision a small pond. For the purpose of discussing watercraft positioning, we must imagine a much larger lake, 20 to 40 acres in the case of the float tubes, canoes, and small prams, to many thousands of acres for bass boats.

Referring to Diagram 3-B, page 56, let's take a boat or float tube around the lake and discuss some of the casting positions. The direction the boat faces is important and demonstrates the position we would prefer, but this can be altered by wind and the position of the sun and shadows. The principles of eliminating places that won't consistently hold largemouths and covering those that will are the objectives. Jump-fishing shad bursts is the only exception to this scheme of structure fishing.

Starting at position Number 1 on the left side of the riprap dam and spillway, position the float tube in close proximity to the dam and turn the tube to cast in each direction. If you are fishing the same area from a boat, the craft should be close to the dam with the bow facing it. The problem with gliding along the length of the dam while staying within casting distance is that the fly spends too much time being dragged through water far too deep and too little time in the fish zone. With better boat positioning, we can fan cast in either direction to cover all the appropriate depths, and keep the fly in that critical fish zone virtually all the way through the retrieve.

Diagram 3-B

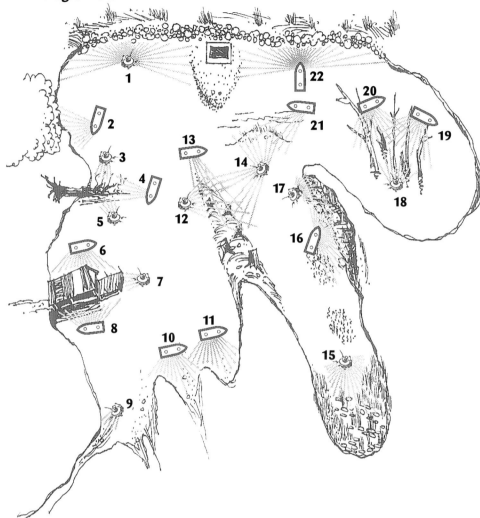

Notice all these positions enable a much more thorough coverage of most pieces of structure. This means the backside, or shore side, of these structures can be fished, as well as the front or inner side. This is particularly evident around the deadfall (positions 3, 4, 5), the dock (positions 6, 7, 8), the submerged point with stumps (positions 12, 13, 14), the aquatic weeds (position 16), the submerged hump (positions 14 and 21), and standing timber (positions 18, 19, 20). When the two of us fish together one of us fishes the inside edge of the structure while the other casts to the outside edge. This tactic helps us determine where the bass are holding or, at least, where they're most active. After discovering which is best, we both concentrate on the productive side and position the boat accordingly. This gives us the best possible chance to hook up with more and larger fish.

As in Diagram 3-A, we recommend eliminating some structure as targets. Depending on weather and season, we apply that principle particularly to fishing reservoirs. One of the great advantages to fishing larger lakes is many areas might qualify as fishable water. Weather, food scarcity, human activity, and sunlight penetration can cause bass to relocate, and in a reservoir they have lots of options available to them.

Delivery Systems

Bank-bound and wading fly-fishers are confined to using stationary casts. For personal watercraft and boat users, the stationary cast is most frequently employed, but it's not the only available choice. Drifting, controlled drifting, and trolling are possible as well.

The purpose of any delivery system is to display the fly to the bass in an enticing manner that causes the fish to strike it. Much has already been written about various stationary casts. Casting experts have written about, and demonstrated on videotape, their methods of casting a tight loop, roll casting, hauling, and double hauling, but it's not our intent to present a casting manual here. If you need to brush up on those techniques, look into their books or videotapes on the subject. The bass fly-caster needs to focus on two practical stationary casts: the open loop cast and the half roll, open loop cast.

Trout fly-fishers mostly cast minute puffs of feathers that are comparatively weightless, but largemouth bass fly-fishermen must accurately place wind-resistant, often heavy, flies. Most of the flies we've recommended, for example, are super-sized and/or laced with lead. In addition, bass fishers frequently must cast sink-tip or full-sinking lines. Throwing tight loops with bass gear creates tsunami-sized splashdowns and worse, the fly can catch its caster in the back of the head. Even when using floating line, the remedy is casting an open loop. The open loop isn't as aesthetically pleasing, and it's far less impressive to observers. It does allow the fly to slow before it reaches water, and the open arc carries it away from the caster.

Casting Modifications

Many are initially attracted to fly-fishing because of its aesthetics. It's fun to watch good fly-casters in action. The pleasing nature of the cast stems largely from the tight loops formed as the fly line changes direction. As an experienced fly-fisher you already cast tight loops, but to lay much larger, less aerodynamic flies with heavier sinking lines accurately and gently on the water you must be able to throw an open loop.

The problem is simple enough. If a size-1/0 fly laced with lead is cast with a tight loop, the weight of the fly overpowers the leader and line and it enters the water at an undesirable rate of speed, which makes a wake-creating splashdown. Solving the problem is easy. Wait long enough on the backcast to straighten the line, then complete the forward cast with a slower than normal rod movement. This lobs the fly into position. The timing of the casting-arm slowdown depends upon the line speed on the backcast, the rod used, and even the speed and direction of the wind. You'll be able to feel and see the open loop this slower rod motion creates, and with a little practice fly control will be comparable to the tight loop cast.

Casting a sink-tip or full-sinking line is more difficult only because its submerged section is harder to pick up from the water. Traditionally, fly-casters have stripped all but a few feet of these lines from the water before the pickup. As a result, several false casts are necessary before the line can be returned to the fish zone. It's hard work and wastes lots of motion and fishing time.

Casting sinking lines is simple. Rather than strip in most of the line, simply lift the rod tip at a slight angle away from your body and begin a roll cast. This action, however slowly it's performed, brings the fly line toward the surface. As the slack line drops from your rod tip in an arc beside you, push your rod tip forward quickly. Before completion of the roll cast, simply allow the line to straighten in front of you, then pull

Selecting the right delivery system enables the angler to release more and larger bass.

briskly into a back cast followed by an open loop forward cast to deliver the fly. With a little practice, you'll be able to shoot line efficiently and perform what we've come to call the half roll, open loop cast from virtually any casting stance. We use it while standing or sitting in a boat, float tubing, and wading.

Wind is a significant obstacle for bass fly-casters whether the destination is prairie ponds or large impoundments. When casting into the wind, sometimes all that's necessary is lowering the rod tip to cast as near the water's surface as possible where the wind is less forceful. This can be performed in a float tube, canoe, or from the bow of a boat. This is also a time for the tight loop and a crouched position. When using a heavy fly, be prepared to duck as part of the casting movement.

If the wind is at your back, the backcast needs to be performed low to the water. A sidearm backcast is used. Rotate the casting arm upward at the end of the backcast so the wind can assist a high forward cast to carry the line and fly to its target.

If the wind blows from the same side as your casting arm, a cross-body cast can be employed from a standing position with single hauls to increase line speed.

Fan Casting

Fan casting is simply casting to several targets from the same position. Theoretically, thorough coverage of all nearby fishing structure would involve casts in an arc from left to right. If the angler stood at the end of a narrow pier, casts would be made to targets in a nearly 360-degree arc.

Fan casting is used to test structures for the portions that are bass hangouts. Another application of fan casting occurs when a bass swirls around, but misses, the fly. It might be more productive to cast to one of the fan-casting targets away from the area before recasting to the now quiet water. If the fly is recast to the same spot right away, the bass can be spooked by the strangeness of a repeated disturbance. After a reasonable interval it might strike the missed meal.

Drifting, Controlled Drifting, and Trolling

In any of the crafts we've discussed, drifting involves utilizing the speed and direction of the wind to blow the vessel over, by, or through structure. Normally this involves using a heavier fly and sink-tip or full-sinking line.

Controlled drifting is but one tiny step further. If you drift off course, use your locomotion (force fins, oars, trolling motor) to make the correction. Inevitably, drifting must evolve into controlled drifting. Winds just aren't that reliable or consistent.

If there is a particularly uncooperative wind or no wind at all, trolling is the remedy. Trolling speeds should be very slow and controlled to stay on the targeted structure. This is a particularly good delivery system for the submerged point and the submerged hump shown in Diagram 3-B. These areas can be drifted, control drifted, or trolled in crisscrossing patterns up, down, and across each piece of structure as long as there's enough depth to permit maneuvers without spooking fish.

Great bass can be caught from small waters by careful bank stalkers.

Trolling and controlled drifting are presentations pioneered in this country by Maine guides more than a century ago. They're a great way to cover a lot of water and present the fly well in the process. There are several nuances that facilitate success.

First, point the rod tip at a 30-degree angle or less away from the fly. We've watched lots of trollers, mostly spin-fishermen, who pointed their rods at right angles to their lures. This puts a very unnatural bend in a fly rod and can cause the rod to be severely taxed when a good fish hits the fly. By pointing the rod tip mostly at the fish the angler is able to control the hook-set. Still, it's not a good idea to point the rod tip directly at the fly because the impact of the strike is absorbed entirely by the tippet. Even a modestly sized fish separates the angler from his terminal tackle under that circumstance.

Second, it's important to control the speed of the troll or drift. Speed, or lack of it, depends on the depth of the desired presentation, which in turn depends on the weight of the fly and line. It's a good idea to vary the speed by trolling at one speed, then accelerate or turn off the motor. By increasing the speed for a short burst, the fly appears to be escaping. It's important to realize however, the increased speed draws the fly toward the surface so the tactic necessitates a slowdown to allow the fly to resettle. An unweighted fly trolled at a fast pace drags along just beneath the surface and accounts for few fish. Changing speeds causes the fly to hop along or undulate at the desired depth. Alternating short bursts from the motor, followed by slowing the boat, should be performed in a predictable rhythm. Just as in the stripping technique used by the stationary caster, this enables the predator to focus on predictable movements and intercept them.

Flies and lines must be chosen with care for the purpose of trolling or drifting. It further advances our earlier statement about the situational nature of flies. It would be ineffective to troll an unweighted marabou streamer over a creek channel with 12 feet of depth on a floating line with a 7 1/2-foot leader. Conversely, we wouldn't troll a lead-laced, size-3/0 Lefty's Deceiver on full-sinking line over the top of a bed of emergent milfoil that extends within 2 feet of the surface. Fly color, size, represented prey, weight, speed, and action should all be carefully chosen to match the fishing situation.

Fly Animation

Usually, some line or rod manipulation is required to cause the fly to interest bass. Line manipulation involves either stripping or the hand-twist retrieve.

After the fly hits the water and before you begin the retrieve on all subsurface flies, count the fly down to the depth you want to fish. For surface flies, including floater/divers and diving lipped flies, immersing the rod tip 1 to 3 inches sometimes allows greater control. Poppers perform more consistently and diving flies penetrate deeper into the water column, especially if there's some surface chop. The critical factors for surface fishing are maintaining straight line from the fly to the rod tip and removing unwanted slack line immediately. If the rod tip is below the surface, remember hook-setting is dependent upon moving line quickly using a long strip rather than moving the rod tip. To strip the fly, pin the line to the rod with your rod hand and pull the length of the line you wish to retrieve. It's a good practice, depending on the type of fly used and bait source imitated, to start with slow, short strips. Two inches is about right. Always allow mid-depth and deep-water flies to resettle back to the desired zone before resuming the stripping process. The strip always brings a submerged fly up toward the surface.

If the fish are unmoved by slow, 2-inch strips, try quick, darting strips. If that doesn't work, try strips of 4 inches, 6 inches or a foot or more. Remember the further the fly is stripped, the longer it takes to resettle.

The hand-twist retrieve is equally simple. Lay your line hand across the line just in front of the reel and grasp it between the thumb and forefinger. Rotate your hand counterclockwise forming a small loop. Grasp the end of the line coil between the thumb and forefinger with the line hand. Rotate your hand back to the original position and repeat the process until the retrieve is completed. Although the hand-twist serves to slow our retrieves when there's a tendency to fish too quickly, most of the time we prefer the strip method.

Stripping and pausing, or twisting and pausing, can be varied to show the bass a different rhythm that can increase their interest. Strip, strip, pause for example, or varying the length of the pause can add the right movement to tempt otherwise reluctant bass.

Fly lines, and ultimately flies, follow the tip of the rod. By changing the direction and angle of the rod tip, we can cause the fly to behave in an erratic manner. This is true whether we're fishing on the surface or into the water column. There are some interesting applications of change-of-direction retrieves.

Spin-fishermen utilize rod-tip change of directions on surface plugs and call the maneuver "walking the dog." The same rod-tip movement can be employed by long rodders. It's especially useful in lily pads or other emergent vegetation with pockets large enough to maneuver a surface fly or floater/diver. It gives the fly the appearance of taking evasive action to avoid freshwater's most efficient predator, and largemouth bass react to potential prey escaping them. We've often had them charge a change-of-direction fly to inhale it with live minnows still in their mouths.

The "change-of-direction" retrieve is accomplished by moving the rod tip in different directions on subsequent strips. To perform it, start by extending the rod tip at an extreme angle to the right. Strip the line, causing the popper to move as far along that path as you want, before pointing the rod tip to the extreme left. Continue stripping as the fly proceeds in a new direction. This demonstrates the radical possibilities of the popper's tracking path. By moving the rod tip, and, consequently, changing the angle of the retrieve, it's easy to see the infinite possibilities. Extending leader lengths, making short casts, and using elongated surface flies like pencil poppers facilitate the process.

Changing directions with subsurface flies is equally effective. We frequently employ the tactic of bumping or banging a heavy fly into dock posts, rocks, riprap, stumps, and even vegetation. Cast beyond the obstruction and allow the fly to sink to the desired level, then move the rod tip as much as 90 degrees so any retrieve causes the fly to bump into the structure. The louder the bump, the better. Remember the bass's super-sensitive lateral line? The noise might just cause the fish to investigate. After the collision, point the rod tip in the opposite direction and strip vigorously. Longer leaders and shorter casts will make the change-of-direction retrieve easier to perform.

Hang Ups

Fishing structure means catching structure often. Hang-ups are frustrating, but most can be remedied with roll casts to free the hook. Creating some slack line, then shaking the rod might work if the distance from the fly to the rod tip is short.

Bass guides use long-handled lure retrievers for hooks firmly attached to deep structure. Cutting several feet off the tips of fly lines can be avoided by keeping this simple tool handy in the boat.

Hook-Setting

For years, bass fishermen have recommended setting the hook with as much force as humanly possible. The tactic was justified, in their view because the species' tough jaws are so difficult to penetrate. While the outside of a bass's mouth is tough and bone-like, the inside is mostly soft tissue.

The hook-set, under normal conditions, need not be excessively forceful. It only needs to be quick and firm. It's best for big bass, however, to set the hook more than once. Largemouth bass's penchant for head-shaking leaps can wallow out the fly's point of penetration and the fish can be lost. The timing of second and third hook-sets should not occur while the bass is running toward you, but if it's running away or deeper into the water column additional quick, firm hook-sets can be the difference between glimpsing the bass of a lifetime and landing it.

More fish have been lost due to slack line than any other reason. In bass fishing, keeping the rod tip low near the surface and vigilantly removing slack are critical to setting the hook. Although it's fundamental, another reminder can't hurt. With every cast, give yourself enough leverage to get a good hook-set.

Chapter 4

Fishing the Shallows

It's not an exaggeration to state more than 95 percent of all fly rod-caught bass are taken from shallow water. Despite the obvious limitations of the practice it's easy to understand any angler's preoccupation with the upper layer of the water column.

Shallow is a relative term dependent on the water's overall size and clarity and subsequent sunlight penetration. It can range from a couple of feet to more than 8 in extreme cases, but for the purpose of definition we define "shallow" as extending from the surface to a depth of 4 feet.

Any of the rod and reel combinations previously discussed serve well, but expected casting distances, wind conditions, and thickness of the targeted cover should determine selection. Floating lines are employed most of the time here, but spare spools with sinking lines serve a purpose in the shallows, too.

Leaders may be 4 to 9 feet, knotless, and tapered, with leader tips of 8- to 20-pound test. Tip size must be matched with the weight and wind resistance of the fly. If the tip is too light, the fly flops about out of control and the resulting poor casting timing creates inaccuracy. If it's too heavy, the fly's action suffers. When mismatches occur, it's a mistake to continue to fish the bad marriage. It just doesn't make good sense to limit your catch with poor leader selection.

A bass's eyes are set high on its head. This enables it to choose lies that permit upward vision. Its eyes allow binocular vision in front of its nose as well as great peripheral vision. Each eye moves independently of the other. Shallow environments offer a good opportunity to capitalize on the bass's vision, but it's important to realize very muddy or obstruction-filled water can inhibit its view.

It might seem advantageous if the fish can readily see your presentation. It isn't. A bass is much more able to detect your fly's phoniness, and almost certainly is warier due to the dangers associated with shallow water from its days as a yearling. Its self-preservation instincts are well developed from all the near misses by avian and aquatic predators.

Even when involvement in the spawning ritual alters the bass's normal caution, shallow water should be approached carefully. Standing in the bow of a boat in bright clothing creates an alarming distraction. Despite dressing appropriately, our body, the rod, and even the fly line's moving shadow spook fish. A quiet, stealthy approach that takes the sun's position into account is another important detail anglers need to consider.

Topwater Flies

Of the surface flies, the obvious and most popular choice for topwater bass is the popper. Something capable of floating on the surface that can be manipulated to make an audible disturbance that imitates some hapless creature floundering and struggling wildly triggers heart-stopping strikes.

Most effective poppers are constructed of cork, closed-cell foam, and deer hair. Foam poppers are generally lighter and more wind resistant. There are great differences in quality, even in commercial poppers. We've purchased some that floated on their sides or didn't sit in the water properly, which affected their ability to pop efficiently. Look for those with cupped faces, durable lacquer coatings, and rubber legs. All poppers present some delivery problems because they catch a lot of air on the forward cast. Foam poppers pop least consistently, but those with weed guards can be pulled over vegetation that snags other flies. Deer-hair poppers have flattened heads, which push water and create a "pop" or gurgle. When wet, they sit in, rather than on, the water, which gives them a more lifelike appearance. Although some fly-casters claim fish more readily accept deer hair's softer, more natural texture, we've never noted any appreciable difference between body materials in their appeal to bass. Casting light, bulky deer hair is like trying to throw a headless badminton birdie, and rods with fast tips are recommended.

In foam, deer hair and cork, patterns, we prefer chartreuse, yellow, or white as the dominant colors of our poppers because they're easily visible to us. We carry some in black and purple, however, because they present a stronger silhouette to the fish when viewed against the backdrop of cloudy skies. Size choices depend largely on the size of the water. More diminutive waters require smaller sizes-4 and -6 flies, and big lakes demand size 2/0 or larger. Frog colors are also good, but match their size to real ones in the area.

Deer-hair bugs tend to soak up water and look bedraggled after several casts. Terry Tanner, Bass Pro Shops Outdoor World Fly Fishing Specialist, found a method of making them last through an entire outing. After he ties spun deer-hair bass bugs, he carefully rubs Orvis Hy-Flote over the entire fly and dries it with a hand-held blow dryer, then repeats the process. He finds he can fish the same twice-dressed bug all day, and even after catching several bass it will continue to float high and dry.

Another type of surface fly, called a "slider," looks similar to a popper but performs the opposite function. Instead of resisting the water it's pulled through, the reversed cork head or pointed shape of the trimmed deer-hair body causes it to glide quietly through the water like a field mouse, frog, or other prospective meal. Sliders are more aerodynamic in shape, much easier to cast, and come in an array of materials, colors, and sizes.

Large, winged deer-hair flies like the original Henshalls are neither poppers nor sliders, so they deserve a category all their own. They're called "wakers." Flies that imitate frogs, mice, or snakes, for example, are fished using strips to create a wake. The large, usually deer hair, wings of a Henshall stick out at a 90-degree angle from its body. The fly gives the appearance of a huge insect or small bird that's fallen into the water, and, despite its efforts, just can't get airborne again. Although any surface fly can be used to create a wake, wakers are bulky flies that don't "pop" or dive, and sit in, rather than on, the water.

Sponge bugs are surface flies with closed-cell foam bodies that imitate large terrestrials. Dragonflies, damselflies, crickets, and grasshoppers land on the tops of emergent vegetation and sometimes wind up as bass food. Their light weight enables them to be presented very softly and makes them a good choice for skittish bass. Fly shops and mail order catalogs offer a good variety, but look for those with rubber legs to enhance their action.

The Need For Weedlessness

Lots of fly-fishers dislike weed guards claiming weedless translates to fishless. Any weed guard we ever used does seem to cause some fish to expel the offering with lightning speed, so we advise not using one anytime you can avoid it. If you're fishing dense wood structure or tangled brush piles, however, weed guards are a fact of life. There are several viable options, but the conventional ones are: trimmed deer hair that's part of the fly's body, a straight piece of monofilament, the monofilament loop, and the commercially available wire weed guard.

Monofilament weed guards should consist of mono heavy enough to prevent the hook point from catching on a limb or branch, but light enough to avoid fishlessness as often as possible. Twenty-pound-test monofilament generally gets this duty on our flies. The mono should be attached at the hook eye and lashed to the shank well into the hook bend. Some tiers use a double mono weed guard positioned on either side of the hook point.

A wire weed guard is a doubled strand of thin wire tied in at the hook eye, sometimes extending through the eye, that's bent at a 45-degree angle from the hook shank. The wire extends below the hook point for the weedless effect. It's not perfect, but it's light, doesn't interfere with the fly's action, and keeps the fly from hang-ups most of the time. The drawback is wire weed guards aren't easy to find, and several sizes must be kept on hand.

Topwater Tactics

There are few differences, and many similarities, in manipulating each kind of surface fly. For poppers, there are two methods from which to choose: (1) short strips of the line, or (2) simultaneous strips while moving the rod tip. Better control that results in the "pop" with the least forward movement can be achieved by manipulating line only. This can be a tremendous advantage, because it allows the fly-fisher to keep his fly closest to the desired cover. The disadvantage to this method is the retrieve must be accomplished in a straight line. The advantage of the rod-manipulated "pop" is that it can become part of a complete retrieve that changes directions erratically or maneuvers around stickups to prevent hanging up. If there's some surface chop, but no obstructions such as surface moss, stick the rod tip an inch or two into the water to get consistent pops without long line strips. If a strike occurs while the rod tip is submerged, the hook-set must be made using a strong line strip. Attempting to set the hook by lifting the rod in the traditional fashion causes it to bow, which weakens the hook-set.

Poppers can be retrieved quickly in a series of loud, nearly continuous "pops," subtle plops punctuated by long pauses or any degree of speed between the two. Add the tracking maneuvers to speed-control and the possibilities are endless. The type of cover should determine the tracking. If the fly must come to the rod along the edge of a weedbed, for instance, a line-manipulated retrieve is best. If the tracking line is a minefield of tree branches, a rod-manipulated change-of-direction retrieve is clearly better. With either it's important to keep the rod tip low and constantly remove slack line.

Unless the bass are in a rare chasing mood, start with a subtle, slow retrieve, but don't stick with a loser. Vary your strips until you find what works. It's important to develop a predictable rhythm with your retrieve. The "pop" should come at regular intervals, as should any direction change. Why? Because it's easier for an ambush predator to lock into the fly's predictable rhythm and take a path that intercepts the fly.

Sliders can be retrieved using the same tracking and speed controls. It's helpful to visualize what prey the fly can be mistaken for by bass. Observing nature's accidental swimmers enhances fly manipulations.

Hard-bodied poppers, sliders, and floater/divers with no appendages and short tails can be "skipped" under docks, walkways, and boathouses so the retrieve can begin in the deepest shadows. A sidearm cast allows the fly to hit the water at the edge of the targeted overhanging structure and causes it to skip across the surface a bit farther before coming to rest. The cast works on the same principle as tossing a flat rock across a pool of water, but don't expect the multiple skips you enjoyed as a kid.

Winged deer-hair "wakers" and sliders can be worked in a nearly stationary manner that can be extremely effective. We call it "quivering." By keeping the rod tip very low and carefully removing all slack, the fly is responsive to the slightest rod movement. Try wiggling the rod tip from side to side rapidly and stripping line only slightly to remove slack. This technique can be lethal on reluctant fish in a neutral feeding mood watching the fly's progress. Quivering the fly can be incorporated into a series of coordinated and predictable movements in the same retrieve.

Change-of-direction retrieves duplicate the successful bait-casting technique known as "walking the dog." Spin-casters usually throw stick baits for this because the length of the lure accentuates its change of direction. Fly-rodders can utilize the retrieve as well by changing their conventional bullet-head poppers to pencil poppers. Pencil poppers are especially handy for dodging stickups without hanging up because their elongated, slender bodies are much easier to maneuver in tight quarters.

The most innovative surface pattern we've seen is Michael Verduin's Ball-Joint Popper. The summer ponds and stock tanks near his Texas home became choked with moss and weeds, so he needed a fly that maintained action after a short strip was terminated or with no strip at all. To fish the Ball-Joint Popper, strip or quiver the round-trimmed deer-hair ball, then let it rest as splayed hackle feathers, attached by a ring, continue to wiggle seductively on the surface. It's a combination of movements that provokes ol' bucketmouth into attacking. When the fly is used as a waker, the tail performs between line strips. Verduin's

Ball-joint Popper is effective in a variety of color patterns. Here's the recipe and tying instructions:

Verduin's Ball-Joint Popper

Hook: Tiemco 8089 or equivalent, size 6

Thread: A Flymaster +

Tail (kickers): 4 olive grizzly rooster hackles

Collar: Folded olive schlappen hackle

Rear Joint: .014 stainless wire leader

Weed Guard: 20-pound hard type mono

Front Joint: 20-pound hard type mono

Body: Spun or stacked deer body hair in white, yellow, olive, and light olive

Tail Section: Cut a 3-inch piece of .014 stainless wire. Create an oval by sticking both tag ends in the vice, taking care not to crease the oval. Stick a 3/16-inch diameter shaft, such as a large nail or small Phillips screwdriver thru the loop. Twist clockwise, pulling away from the vise jaws, creating a loop slightly larger than the shaft. Cut the twisted wire shaft, leaving a 1/4-inch shaft sticking out from the loop, and put the loop's end in the vise with the loop horizontal to the ground. Wrap a small ball of thread at the end of the twisted wire and tie in 2 pairs of kickers, splayed. Fold an olive schlappen feather, and tie in by the tip end, wrapping to the loop, to form a collar. Tie off and cement.

Body Section: Tie the weed guard mono down the far side of the hook curve, covering approximately 40 percent of the hook bend, then back up stopping just short of the straight portion of the hook shank. Cement the wraps. Flatten the end of a 3-inch piece of mono and tie in at the tail of the hook shank. Place the loop of the tail section over the end of the mono. Pull the mono forward, forming a loop approximately the same size as the tail section loop by tying the folded mono on top of the previous tie-in. Clip the excess mono, tie off, and cement heavily. Retie, and spin or stack a deer-hair body, using five to six stages, and clip the body to a sphere or ball. Bring the weed guard mono up the near side of the hook, just behind the eye making 5 to 6 wraps of thread. Pull the tag end of the mono up

accustomed to those sounds. They wait for and rely upon them. In fact, without them bass would be forced to forage more frequently for food rather than ambush it.

Each presentation involves the change-of-direction retrieve. Rock-banging, for instance, can be accomplished by fishing progressively down a rock-lined shore. A riprap area is a good example. By casting parallel to the rocks, then pointing the rod tip toward the rocks and stripping briskly, the hook eye and head make a clicking sound as they contact the riprap. By aiming the rod tip toward open water and stripping again, the fly imitates escaping prey. Rock-banging can be a lethal technique (Diagram 4-A).

Several seasons ago, we chose a gorgeous autumn day to revisit a favorite lake that had produced some great bass for us years before. The small impoundment had an unusually long riprap dam. We cast to shallow cover in several coves, and probed the depths of each main lake

Diagram 4-A

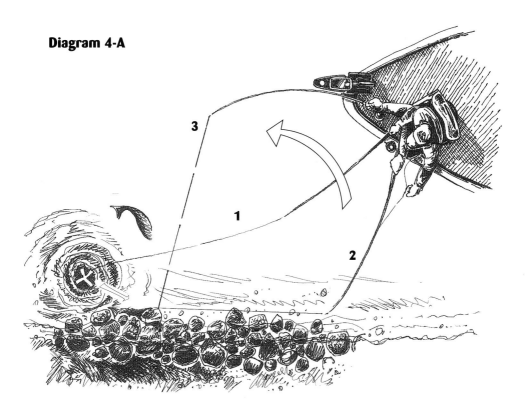

point without moving a fish of respectable size. We were about to conclude the water's glory days were gone when we cast along the riprap on the way back to our vehicle. It was like flipping a switch. We tied on hard-headed floater/divers and worked the entire length of the dam three times before the fading sunlight brought the season's coolness to the landscape. With amazing consistency, flies that clicked into the rocks before we scurried them away brought charging strikes. Together we caught and released over 30 bass. Many measured between 14 and 16 inches, and one measured just over 20. We're convinced the bass were lying in wait in the depths beyond the rocks and responded only when they heard our rock-banging. Duplicating the tactic since has produced some outstanding catches.

Impoundments near our home are loaded with wood structure. Logjams, stumps, standing timber, and docks provide excellent bass cover if the fish have immediate access to deep water. One of our favorite shallow-water tactics is "stump-knocking." To accomplish it, cast beyond the targeted stump or dock piling and angle the rod so the path of the fly must intersect it. As soon as contact is made, point the rod tip toward open water and repeat the stripping process.

"Veggie-bumping" involves contacting a weedline. Milfoil, coontail, and other soft aquatic plants are perfect for this tactic. The principle is the same as rock-banging and stump-knocking, but the actual practice has an interesting feature. Once the fly bumps into the thick forest of weeds, the hook frequently catches a stem or a bunch of leaves. This enables the angler to pull the fly free, and, in the process, gently shake the submerged forest. The bass is alerted that its neighborhood has been invaded. Sharp hooks are an important detail that needs more attention in general, but in veggie-bumping it's extremely important. If the hook isn't razor sharp and the tippet is too supple, the weeds are simply dragged back to the rod fishless. This tactic actually inspired the others, and we had numerous bass hookups after accidental weed encounters before we realized we should repeat the process.

Structure-bumping wears flies, knots and leaders. Even veggie-bumping manages to undo thread-wrapped fly heads and stretch monofilament beyond its limits. Check leaders for nicks and knots for strength often to prevent losing a great bass to extraordinary wear and tear.

Non-Floaters For Shallow Water

Thin-water fishing shouldn't be limited to floating flies. Fishing shallow usually means imitating the looks and actions of baitfish, crayfish, or salamanders.

Young bluegills, crappie, and perch are available to shallow bass. All should be fished in erratic strips accompanied by frequent changes of direction. There are lots of fly choices to fill the bill from simple, impressionistic bucktail and marabou streamers to lipped creations with built-in action.

Crayfish are a favorite food source for shallow-lurking bass. We use the simplest impressionistic pattern possible that we call a "Woollie." Most crayfish patterns are too complicated and call for separated pincers, but the young crayfish the Woollie represents aren't much of a threat in fighting posture. The marabou tails we favor look like real crayfish when their pincers are tucked together as they take flight. We use lots of lead to get the fly down to the bottom, and if our pattern kicks up a little silt trail, so much the better. Here's the simple pattern:

Ginger Woollie

Hook: TMC 5262 sizes 4 and 6
Thread: Brown pre-waxed monocord
Tail: Several strands of copper Krystal Flash surrounded by ginger
  marabou
Underbody: 20 to 25 wraps of .030 lead wire or the equivalent
Body: Tan wool yarn
Head: Brown thread
Note: This tan color represents the soft-shelled stage of crayfish whose
  protective carapaces have not yet hardened. Although they're favored
  by bass, we've also had good success with an olive version of the same
  fly. Woollies are so easy to tie they make a good pattern for beginners.

One of the most overlooked shallow-water imitations is the salamander. Particularly during the spawning process, sallies seek out nesting bass and feed voraciously on the eggs. A salamander fly that swims enticingly through a bass spawning colony draws the attention of the nearby bass in the same way crows rally to attack an owl.

Our own version is a pattern we originated called "Wilson's Jointed Sally." Here's the recipe:

Wilson's Jointed Sally (purple)

Hooks: Trailing Hook: TMC 8089, size 10; Front Hook: TMC 8089, size 6

Weed Guard: 25-pound stiff mono on both hooks

Thread: Purple pre-waxed monocord

Tail Section Construction:

Tail: Small purple twister tail attached with curl extending upward

Legs: Triple strand of purple round rubber hackle tied in at mid-shank to extend from the shank. A knot tied in the last 1/2 inch of rubber hackle simulates the feet

Body: Purple Long Flash Chenille

Head: Purple E-Z Shape Sparkle Body

Eyes: Medium red barbell with black pupil

Front Hook Construction:

Connector: Wrap a piece of 25-pound-test monofilament to the top of the hook shank, thread it through the hook eye of the trailing hook allowing the loop to provide free movement

Body: Purple Long Flash Chenille

Legs: Duplicate the triple round rubber hackle legs and feet at mid-shank of the front hook

Eyes: Yellow barbell eyes

Head: Purple E-Z Sparkle Body

Note: We've also had success with this pattern in chartreuse, brown, and black.

Fishing Sallies is one situation in which we sometimes use full-sinking line to fish a shallow-water fly. Floating line causes the fly to rise from the bottom toward the surface on the retrieve (Diagram 4-B). Sometimes this is desirable, but when it's not, we use full-sinking line to

Diagram 4-B

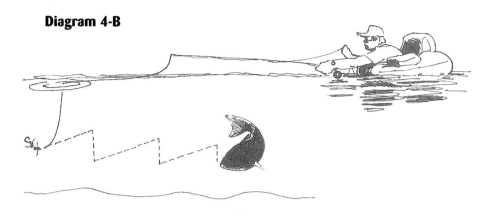

keep the fly crawling along the bottom as if it was searching for bass eggs (Diagram 4-C).

When bass are chasing shad or other baitfish in the shallows, one of the best fly choices is the Cowen's Coyote. Henry Cowen hails from Atlanta, Georgia, and frequents Lake Sidney Lanier, but the Coyote got its start in Connecticut in both fresh and salt water. The front-mounted spinner causes it to fish like the spin casters' Roadrunner. It performs well in other situations, too, but it adapts nicely to the shallows because the hook point rides upright. Here's the recipe:

Diagram 4-C

Cowen's Coyote

Hook: Tiemco 811S, size 1/0

Spinner: #12 barrel swivel tied right behind the hook eye. Attach a size-1 split ring and size-00 Colorado spinner blade

Eyes: Size 5/32 Real Eyes

Belly: White Zonker strip extending 1 1/2 inches from hook bend and impaled on a 30-pound mono spike tied to extend from the bend for approximately 3/8 inch. Burn the mono end to prevent the Zonker strip from coming off. The spike prevents the Zonker strip from interfering with the rotation of the spinner blade

Back: Several strands of pearl Flashabou and purple bucktail covered by 4 to 5 strands of olive bucktail

Commercially available flies for shallow water include marabou streamers in sizes 6 to 1/0 (we prefer white or yellow), big hair-wing streamers in sizes 6 to 1/0 (we prefer brown over white and red over white), and size-4 Woolly Buggers that incorporate rubber hackle.

Targeting Shallow Structure

As we approach our fishing destinations, structures above the waterline become obvious casting targets. Selecting the best of them and presenting productive flies, then, becomes the dilemma. Although it's impossible to describe every fishing situation, here are some common shallow-water structures, flies, and proven retrieves.

Emergent vegetation, such as lily pads or cattails, is an obvious place to begin fishing with poppers and floater divers when the sun is low on the horizon. Evenings in the shallows with fly rods and surface flies are legendary, but sunrises and overcast skies can offer equally exciting action. Look for indentations in the outer edges and cast to those first, then cast to larger open pockets. If there are no indentations and pockets, cast along the length of the vegetation as near the edge as possible. Sparse weeds that resemble loose mats on the water's surface can be fished with lightweight weedless surface flies crawled across the tops and paused in small open areas. Weedless poppers and sliders, floater/divers, terrestrials such as dragonflies, and frog imitations work best. Wet flies with weed guards, such as match-the-minnow streamers,

Cowen's Coyote has its roots in salt water, but it's a versatile largemouth offering.

including young bluegill, crappie, and perch imitations, large Woolly Bugger variations, and leech imitations, are good choices.

Floating vegetation is fished in the same manner. Rafts of floating vegetation, if they are large enough to provide dense shade, can be fished later in the morning and earlier in the evening. Bass locate underneath and can dash out to grab a meal. If there are points jutting from the main raft, try using the wind to drift mid-depth flies beneath them. Filamentous weeds can also become floating rafts, but fishing them is confined to the edges.

Vegetation that grows near the water's surface but doesn't emerge is another target for surface flies. Areas with hydrilla or other soft-stemmed aquatic plants hold bass in their cool, dark recesses where fish can ambush passing prey. Breaklines where underwater plants meet emergent ones can be the most productive locations. Noisy fly animations and veggie-bumping with poppers and gurgling floater/divers are good techniques for subsurface vegetation. There's also enough unobstructed water surface to use wakers effectively.

Although its roots can anchor in 20 feet of water, milfoil presents a shallow fishing target. Its long stems can reach the surface, and it can be fished in the same manner as other, shallower vegetation. Large bass often suspend in milfoil only a few inches from its tops. Poppers, wakers, and floater/divers should be manipulated vigorously to attract the bass's attention. Streamers that produce solid hits in other vegetation work in milfoil, too.

When a creek enters a river, areas of slack water are sometimes created at the creek's mouth. Slack water near current is a prime location for large bass. Fishing crosscurrents is difficult because moving water sweeps fly lines into prevailing currents and fly control becomes impossible. Floater/divers, such as Wiggle Minnows, that imitate injured baitfish are excellent choices, and, if the slack water is large enough to avoid currents, poppers can also be productive. Streamers with spinners, standard hair-wing and marabou streamers, and Woolly Buggers can be fished effectively here.

When a creek enters still water there are usually eddies on either side of the creek's mouth. Bass can locate in slack water just beyond the eddies where food can wash to them. Cast to the eddy's edge, if it can be identified, and bring the fly across slack water. Floater/divers are often better than poppers in this location, but wakers and mouse or frog imitations work, too.

Stumps in shallow water are good targets for poppers, sliders, and floater/divers. Hardheaded floater/divers for stump-knocking are also good choices. Frog and baitfish imitations, Woolly Bugger variations, and leeches are the wet-fly selections.

Rootwads are best fished on their downstream sides where there are current breaks. Cast topwater flies or baitfish imitations so they can be retrieved along all the slack water provided by the rootwad and its trunk. There can be another stump-knocking opportunity, too.

If logjams have exposed sections, fish irregularities along their faces. Poppers are especially effective when they're cast into pockets and fished tight to wood. Quivering techniques are advisable so flies remain on the targets most of the time. Weedless streamers, Woolly Buggers, and leeches also trigger strikes.

Overhanging brush requires sidearm casts to place flies underneath. Quivering techniques and short strips work best because such shady areas are usually small. Insect larvae and mature insect imitations can be most successful under this structure, but mice, frogs, and snakes are good choices, too. Poppers, wakers, and floater/divers that merely imitate the action of natural prey all work well beneath overhanging brush. Weedless minnow imitations are also good choices.

Boat docks are common targets for topwater fishing. Cast into their shade or tight to their supports. Give attention to attending walkways, especially shaded corners where they meet the shore, if the water is more than a foot deep. Approach back corners with care and cast softly. Any dramatic commotion can send bass to deeper water. The corner where the walkway meets the dock is also a good casting target. Duck blinds are fished in essentially the same manner as boat docks. Cast along the edges, shaded sides, and under plank walkways.

Submerged fence rows, especially those in ponds, can be good topwater locations. Cast to the shallowest corner first, and work the fly along the fenceline over or into progressively deeper water. Recognize fences have two corners at each shoreline and cast to all of them. Poppers and weedless frog imitations are good choices.

It's easy to understand the enormous popularity of shallow bass. The explosiveness of a surface strike has addicted generations of bass aficionados. Hooked shallow bass fight especially well in confined quarters, making acrobatic leaps with much of their bulldogging and thrashing style fully visible to the excited angler. We're as fascinated with shallow bass as anyone, and probably spend a disproportionate amount of time pursuing them. Still, it's important to recognize bass frequently seek the comfort and protection of deeper water. When they do, we need a whole new bag of tricks.

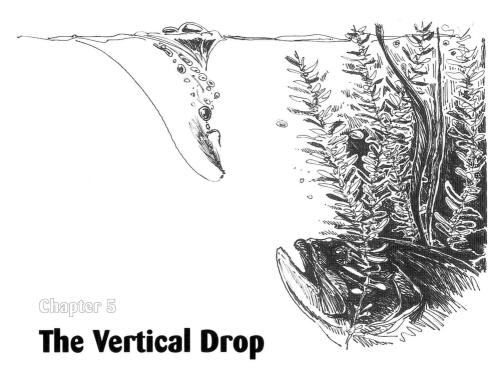

Chapter 5

The Vertical Drop

Nearly every lure and fly ever created was designed to be pulled across or through the water. Both are decidedly horizontal presentations, yet big largemouth bass spend a relatively small amount of time chasing prey. Instead, they take a lie that offers ambush opportunities. They can conceal themselves at the edge of a weedline where there's a view of open water. Crippled, injured, or dying prey fluttering helplessly into their fields of vision are almost certainly offers too good to refuse, but healthy minnows swimming horizontally are only pursued if the bass are hungry. Even then, they instinctively compare the calories derived from the meals to the energy expended in their capture.

Consider also that larger bass don't feed more than once every 3 to 5 days. Only smaller, shallow-hugging largemouths are in constant pursuit of small food. Those that provide the bulk of angling thrills are lazy critters that much prefer to capture one substantial meal, then spend the next several days digesting it while lying nearly motionless peering out at the world from the security of their shelter. That doesn't leave many opportunities for anglers to encounter them, so we need to slant the odds in our favor. One concept does that—much larger flies that pique the interest of well-fed bass. Far more important, however, is the need to place our offerings with the appropriate action right in front of their noses. This need makes casting accuracy extremely important, but also begs the phony meal to drop from the surface into the bass's view.

When fishing for largemouth bass, we have to make some choices. If we want to catch bluegills, other sunfish, and an occasional small bass, then we should fish the shallows with appropriately small flies. In this scenario, we need only focus our efforts exclusively on the pre-spawn through post-spawn periods or sunrises and sunsets. On the other hand, if we want to succeed in catching larger bass, even under adverse conditions, we must recognize the need to present large flies vertically.

Several important factors need to be considered to fish the vertical drop efficiently. First, we need a thorough understanding of the water's bottom contour and structure. Ideally, we could walk about on the bottom of our favorite lake or river making notes about the locations of drop-offs, channels, rock piles, dock pilings, brush, submerged trees, stumps, and vegetation. Obtaining lake maps of large impoundments helps, but we need to know exactly where fish-holding areas are while we're fishing. On small waters we must rely upon visual observations plus experiences from repeated casts. Our efforts are often aided because these miniature bass factories tend to be "what-you-see-is-what-you-get" situations. All the structure is visible—deadfalls, riprap, and weedlines. Frequently, in older ponds a thick layer of silt has erased the breaklines, creek channels, and other bottom structure. Waters large enough to launch a float tube or a boat are another matter. Here, our best tool is a locator. Locators or fish finders come in sizes small enough to mount on a float tube or pack along with a cartop boat. Whether it's a graph or flasher unit doesn't matter as long as the angler understands how to use it and how to interpret what the device shows.

We really don't often find fish on the locator, and then catch them. Almost always, we're looking for bass cover because bass just aren't found in open water with regularity, although there are instances in which some larger male pre-spawners use depressions as staging areas while waiting for warmer water temperatures to beckon them onto the flats to begin the nest-building process.

Diagram 5-A

The second important consideration for fishing the vertical drop is understanding the sink rate of your fly, and, if applicable, sinking fly line. Manufacturers give line sink rates in inches per second. That information should be taken into account in its purchase, but that's not valuable in knowing when your offering is located just above a fly-eating brush pile or how far it might have tumbled down the edge of a weed bank. That knowledge is best acquired by watching the line and fly in clear, obstruction-free water and through fishing experience. A well-practiced angler can make contact with structure and lift the fly away from danger. This practice inevitably causes some lost flies, but it can also account for many more lunkers.

Counting down the fly is a habit all warmwater fly-fishers should acquire because the countdown is an important part of locating the fly in the water column. By counting, "one-thousand-one, one-thousand-two," etc., a sense of the fly's depth can be developed. One angler's count can differ widely from another's, but that doesn't matter. If the count is consistent, and structure contact is made at the count of 8, for example, we know precisely when to begin our retrieve. We'll also be able to determine the bass's depth under prevailing conditions when fish contact occurs at a certain count. That's critical information because we will

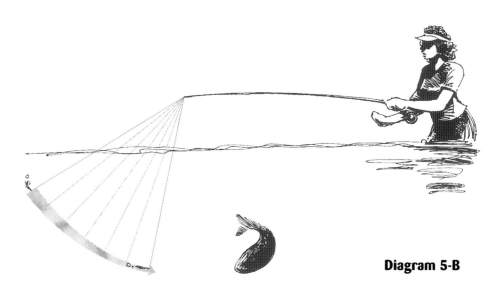

Diagram 5-B

have determined the comfort zone for bass in consideration of water temperature and sunlight penetration and, perhaps, the level of their prey species. Continue to fish at that depth until conditions change and bass contact is made elsewhere in the water column.

Finally, we need to consider the path the fly takes into the water. Fishing a true vertical drop necessitates a slack-line cast (Diagram 5-A). It's slack line that determines the maximum depth of the vertical drop. If there's not enough slack, the fly is forced off course before it bows toward the rod. Bowing has a place in fishing the vertical drop, but if the fly is fished directly below its point of entry it's necessary to provide slack. The technique of bowing, on the other hand, requires the fly's splashdown occur well beyond its intended target. If the line is kept taut, the fly drops in an arc toward the target area (Diagram 5-B). Bowing can be used if we expect bass to be located along a weedline but we don't know their depth. By using a trolling motor to ease along the edge, casts can be made ahead of the boat and allowed to bow back to a point directly beneath the rod. This tactic enables the fly-caster to probe various depths until fish contact reveals where the fish are located.

Although bowing allows the angler to feel the strike, slack-line vertical fishing requires much greater concentration. With this technique, an angler watches for any pull or even slight hesitation to signal the take. Alert anglers frequently set the hook when the fly has made contact with structure, but they also catch more fish.

Most vertical drop situations require sinking lines, so it's necessary to choose rods with that in mind. Leaders can be relatively short; usually 4 to 6 feet suffice, unless the water is exceptionally clear. We try to keep the tippet size light to facilitate the fly's natural action. Tippets of 8- to 12-pound test are best.

Flies For the Vertical Drop

There are a few flies that perform well as they drop vertically through the water column, but not many were actually designed for the specific purpose. Nearly three decades ago we designed a bluegill fly we called "Bully's Bluegill Spider" that's constructed to fall hook bend first so rubber-hackle legs at its head wiggle enticingly on the descent. In fact, nationally recognized fly authority Chuck Tryon, author of *Figuring Out Flies* and creator of the BUBfly, said, "With the exception of ice flies, your Bully's Bluegill Spider is the only fly I know that was actually designed to be fished on the vertical drop."

Usually ice flies are tiny jigs that combine a shiny metal body with marabou so they can be fluttered toward bottom and yo-yoed back to the surface. Fly-fishermen can use them, but their most frequent use is by ice fishermen.

It's astounding that bass fishing's most productive presentation has so few flies created for it. Tiers interested in breaking new ground with flies for the vertical drop need to consider three criteria: (1) the choice of materials, (2) where and how to weight the fly, and (3) how to attach the materials.

Tying materials are important because these flies must create their own action, free of outside manipulation, while falling through the water column. Flexibility can be the key. Rubber hackle, marabou, rabbit strips, soft plastic twister tails, and chamois cloth are examples of materials we've used to give our flies this independent action.

Deciding where and how to weight flies for the vertical drop depends on how the fly is intended to fall. Two possibilities are weighting the fly at the hook eye, and weighting the hook bend. While our list of flies tied for the vertical drop is short, there's one we originated to help fill the void.

Wilson's Bass Bully (white)

Hook: TMC 8089, sizes 2 through 1/0
Thread: White UNI-Stretch
Weed Guard: 20-pound Mason stiff mono
Tail: White twister tail with curl extending upward
Body: White Long Flash Chenille
Weighting: 25 turns of .020 lead wire to build head
Collar: Four strands of clear/pearl-silver-flake round rubber hackle, doubled, tied to extend away from the hook shank 90 degrees
Eyes: Red Hologram eyes 5/32-inch
Head: Pearl E-Z Shape Sparkle Body
Note: Other colors, including black, brown (pumpkin), purple, and chartreuse, have been used successfully.

The Wilson's Bass Bully is weighted at the head, and its rubber hackle and twister tail are activated as it dives head first into the water. Its action doesn't suffer as it's retrieved. While no other flies we know about have been created to perform this function there are several that can be used successfully.

One fly in our arsenal that fishes well on the vertical drop is the Rabbit Strip Leech. Tom Nixon's fur leech is the pattern we use:

Rabbit Strip Leech (Fur Leech) (black)

Hook: Straight eye, wide gap. (We use Tiemco 8089, size 6)
Tail: Black rabbit fur strip, skin-side up
Body: Cross-cut black rabbit fur strip, wrapped over the full length of the hook shank.
Eyes: Silver bead chain or chrome lead eyes with black pupils
Note: We have particular success with this pattern when it's dropped along dock pilings and steep rock bluffs.

Squirrel Spins can be utilized for the vertical drop.

Flies that incorporate a trailing spinner also serve as hook bend/head-weighted vertical drop flies. One is the Thunder-Spin tied by Kentucky Lake guide Ron Kruger:

Thunder-Spin

Hook: Mustad 9672, size 8

Weight: 5 wraps of .020 lead wire

Wing and Head: White marabou tied Thunder Creek style

Gills: Red thread

Trailer: 00 Colorado spinner and swivel added by slipping over the hook barb place and held in place high on the hook bend by wrapping thread above and below its position

Note: Kruger developed the pattern for fishing shad bursts on Kentucky Lake, but it's great when dropped along rock bluffs, weed beds, docks, or anyplace largemouths might be on the lookout for free-falling minnows. We prefer to use Thunder-Spins early in the year when the shad are small.

He also ties the Squirrel Spin, which is similar to, but larger than, the Thunder-Spin. We use Squirrel Spins in early fall on our home lake when school bass, up to about 15 inches long, chase gizzard shad. Follow shad bursts with the trolling motor, and cast to the burst's edges or ahead of the rampaging bass. Fishing the fly on the vertical drop simulates a shad wounded in the attack. Unless one of the school bass pounces on it first, it can drift down to one of the bigger bass following the action to feed opportunistically on the fallout. Here's the recipe:

Squirrel Spin

Hook: TMC 9395, size 4

Head: Red 6/0

Wings: Gray squirrel tail stacked and tied to extend just past the hook bend

Body: Silver Mylar tubing

Trailer: 00 Colorado spinner and swivel slipped over the hook barb with thread wraps above and below its position on the upper hook bend to hold it in place

Note: This fly is also particularly effective when fishing for river largemouths in slow, deep pools.

Another pattern for the vertical drop is the Flap Tail Shad created by Henry Cowen. It was first conceived as a striper pattern but shad-feeding largemouths love them, too. The spinner is attached to flap, rather than spin, which gives it a much different action.

Flap Tail Shad

Hook: Standard saltwater, sizes 4 though 2/0; Tiemco 811S; Mustad 34007; Daiichi 2546

Thread: Danville fine translucent monofilament

Flap Tail: 40-pound-test clear monofilament and a size-00 silver or brass Colorado spinner blade (a willow leaf blade may be substituted in clear water)

Skirt: White marabou and pearl Flashabou

Underbody: Pearl E-Z Body, braided tubing, and peacock herl
Throat: Red E-Z Body braided tubing
Body: Pearl E-Z Body braided tubing, and 5-minute epoxy
Eyes: Small silver prismatic stick-on

There are other head-weighted flies that perform well on the vertical drop, but these are ones we've used successfully.

While our own Bully's Bluegill Spider is an example of a hook-bend weighted vertical drop fly, it's intended for bluegills. Even when it's tied in sizes appropriate for bass, it's not a fly we'd recommend for bass fishing. Again, we know of no hook-bend weighted flies tied for that purpose, but there is one that we've adapted. Tom Nixon's Calcasieu Pig Boat was originally tied for fishing in the same manner as the Arbogast Hawaiian Wiggler, but without added weight. We've tied several Pig Boats weighted with lead wire at the hook bend, which causes the fly to sink tail first. The rubber-hackle tentacles just go crazy on the fly's descent. Drop it next to submerged stumps and among the branches of standing timber. Here's our modified version of Nixon's great fly:

Calcasieu Pig Boat (black, modified)

Hook: Straight eye, heavy wire
Weighting: 10 turns of .030 lead wire tied in at the hook bend.
Body: Black chenille, heavy
Body Hackle: Black, tied in by the butt and palmered
Collar: About 60 strands of black rubber hackle evenly distributed
Head: Black, with a painted yellow eye and red pupil

The Calcasieu Pig Boat, the Flap Tail Shad, and the Rabbit Strip Leech are commercially available through mail-order suppliers and fly shops.

The Great Worm Debate

Over the years we asked lots of fly-fishers, as well as countless bankside philosophers, to define what constitutes a fly. We received a lot of puzzled looks and about as wide a variety of definitions as the number of folks we asked. To many, it doesn't matter much except to the person doing the fishing. Others restricted the definition to exclude some of the flies we've recommended. We understand the conflict. After all, there must be some boundaries. None of us would endorse just any method that's effective. Dynamite works too, but it's clearly outside the rules, so maybe what's needed is some definition. The best we've run across belongs to Chuck and Sharon Tryon, authors of *Figuring Out Flies*. Their take on it is, "a fly is any artificial bait, made at least partly of flexible or pliant materials attached to a hook by any method other than skewering them on it which an angler supposes can entice a fish into putting its mouth around it and which, without an extremely heavy hook or weight added for the sole purpose of making it heavier, can be cast effectively only with a fly rod and line." Theirs is an opinion we greatly respect and their definition is as liberal as any we've heard. There is no doubt, how- ever, conventional bait-casters' plastic worms are not allowed even by the Tryons' accepting definition. Having said that, it's important to point out plastic worms do catch bass and some fly anglers choose to use them.

Over 30 years ago, Tom Nixon wrote about their effectiveness and encouraged their use. He even devoted an entire chapter of *Fly Tying and Fly Fishing for Bass and Panfish* to "Pork Rind and Plastic Worms." Most fly-casters regarded the idea as a violation of the rules. About a quarter of a century later, Texan Jack Ellis had the temerity to suggest Nixon had been right all along. Ellis explained he fished regularly with some excellent bait-casters. He said he could account for his share of fish when the light was low, but when the sun found the water and the bass retreated to the brush and weeds he'd just as well case his rod if he persisted in throwing conventional flies. When he tied on a plastic worm, however, he could hold his own. Again, the idea wasn't warmly received.

Some have suggested this worm controversy is a modern version of the debate between Halford and Skues, who long ago argued in the halls of the London Fly Fishing Club over the unsportsmanlike practice of nymph-fishing for trout. Perhaps. The very independent thinkers who make up our sport will decide the issue. Rules can get in the way of innovation that often benefits us all, but while we wouldn't try to persuade anyone for or against the use of plastic worms we decline their use. There are many alternatives to the plastic worm, and all can be fished weedless in the heaviest cover. As vertical drop flies, they're superior to plastic worms because the materials used in their construction are more flexible. Here are the recipes for our favorites:

Whitlock's Eelworm Streamer

Hook: Salmon wet

Wing: 4 long, narrow yellow-dyed grizzly hackles outside of which are 2 short, wide yellow-dyed grizzly hackles

Eyes: Chromed lead or silver bead chain, tied under hook shank

Body: Black chenille or dubbing

Hackle: Yellow-dyed grizzly, palmered over the chenille

Head: Red thread

Note: Whitlock first tied this fly in 1975 and described it as the fly-rodder's answer to the plastic worm. We fish this one relatively shallow along the edges of weedbeds or over carpets of grass. A weed guard can be included, of course, but unless the vegetation is pretty thick; we use it plain in a variety of colors.

Whitlock's Hare Worm (red)

Hook: Straight eye, wide gap (we use 8089, size 6)

Wing: Long claret rabbit fur strip impaled over the hook point, skin side up, the forward end secured under the hook shank, behind the hook eye. (Claret rabbit strips can be hard to find, so we've substituted red.)

Back: A short strip of red rabbit fur, skin side down, cemented on top and secured behind the eye of the hook

Eyes: Solid plastic (We fine-tune this pattern by using various weights of lead barbell eyes which enable control of its sink rate.)

Note: Experiment with a variety of plastic worm colors on this one. Tackle shop walls are covered with a seemingly infinite selection of plastic worms, but each region of the country seems to have a popular color. We tie in a mono weed guard and use the Hare Worm, especially in heavier sizes, to drop into the toughest cover, such as logjams and brush. If it's temporarily draped over a limb, seesaw it back and forth to create the kind of sound that causes ol' bucketmouth to investigate.

Casting along a shaded wall of weeds is an opportunity to employ the vertical drop.

The Future Of Vertical-Drop Flies

Most of the flies we've listed here weren't created with the vertical drop in mind. They're used for it simply because their weighting method and materials lend themselves well to enticing freefalls in the water. With the exception of our modification of Nixon's Calcasieu Pig Boat, all enter the fish's view head-first.

Quality flies for the vertical drop are in critically short supply. Aside from surface flies and floater/divers, other largemouth bass flies should be tied with consideration of this freefalling water entry. Those even marginally attractive on the drop often catch more bass when the fly falls without imparted action. The reason is clear. Sizeable largemouth bass don't chase their meals very often. Even in relatively shallow areas the vertical drop triggers the strike.

The vertical drop isn't the only presentation necessary in bass fishing, but with few exceptions it's the most reliable for any bass fisher after the spawn. This is especially true for the larger of the species-those beyond 13 or 14 inches.

Evaluate the bass flies you tie and those you purchase. Creative, skilled tiers will soon fill this need with an array of big flies with lots of non-imparted action.

Targeting Structure For the Vertical Drop

The best structures for vertical drop presentations are submerged weeds, stumps, rock formations, and brush. All must be in at least 3 feet of water.

Brush is ideal for the vertical drop. Cast over it and let the fly flutter down, then begin the strip before branch-contact is made. Position so it's possible to cast along a brush line and get 2 or 3 drops on one cast by lifting the rod tip and allowing the fly to resettle. The process might not involve much stripping. If the target is brush along an old creek channel, use tail spinner and twister tail flies, leech patterns (Whitlock's for shallower water), Calcasieu Pig Boats, or any weighted, jig-type fly with tail action and/or rubber hackles.

Wash areas after rains are good targets if sharp drops into deep water accompany them. Toss flies tight to their shorelines, let them sink a foot or two, then lift and strip to drop them into deeper water. Wilson's

Sallies, Woodruff's Swamp Rabbits, Bass Bullies, and large Woolly Buggers are good choices.

In areas of bottom composition changes, choose flies that are good for mid-depth retrieves to take advantage of both vertical drop and mid-depth fishing, such as Calcasieu Pig Boats and E-Z Deceivers (recipe in Chapter 7). If there's notable bottom contrast, gravel next to mud, for example, choose flies with spinners or those with colors that correspond to bass prey likely to be found there.

Choose points that offer some type of additional cover, such as brush, rocks, or stumps. There are numerous boat positions for fishing the vertical drop on points. One good tactic is using the trolling motor to stay within a reasonable casting range of the point's crest. Casts can be made to the shallow portion, and vertically dropped into progressively deeper water. Another option is anchoring the boat on the point's crest to cast to deeper water on three sides. Lift the rod tip and strip to hop the fly.

Creek channels with submerged brush offer excellent opportunities to employ the vertical drop with weedless flies. Use a controlled drift to fish tight to the brush tops with E-Z Deceivers (recipe in Chapter 7) and W.I.T.H. Buggers (recipe in Chapter 6) and focus on the creek's bends. Counting down the fly is critical to preventing hang-ups.

Bluffs are perfect targets for the vertical drop. Wilson's Sallies, Calcasieu Pig Boats, Flap Tail Shads, Cowen's Coyotes, and big Woolly Buggers work well. If it's a deep, rocky bluff, head-weighted worm patterns in dark colors with flexible tails can provoke powerful hits. Position the boat close to the wall and cast along its face. Concentrate on attending structures and bluff shelves. If the bluff has a series of ledges, try hopping flies from one to the next. If the bluff slopes gradually into deep water the boat should be positioned a comfortable cast away from the bluff's base so the fly can be hopped from shallow to deep water. If there are undercuts in a bluff's rock base, as there are in some strip pits and canyon lakes, the vertical drop is a good presentation.

In standing timber, the first order of business is to determine how far the limbs project from the tree. If the fish are in 6 feet of water in extended branches that are 10 to 20 feet above the tree's base, cast to

The vertical drop is the most logical way to present flies to an ambush predator.

within 10 feet of the trunk from 40 feet away and count the fly down. The locations of the branches won't be known, so flies must be weedless. If you have the benefit of a locator, troll over the places where you expect to find extended branches. This might necessitate moving in a circle several feet from the tree's trunk to quickly determine if bass are located there. Bring the fly toward the outer branches with a lift, strip, and drop retrieve. Tail spinners and twister tails help to slow the speed of the drop. Set the hook even on slight hesitations. If the fish are located in extended branches in relatively deep water, 8 feet or more, for example, the most productive presentation is yo-yoing. To perform it, use a heavy fly with the boat positioned directly above the fish. Count the fly down to the correct depth, then lift and drop the rod tip repeatedly to entice the bass.

Around stumps, drop Calcasieu Pig Boats or other weighted flies with rubber legs to the shaded sides. Woodruff's Swamp Rabbits, leeches, and Bass Bullys are good, too. Select weighted worm flies according to the depth of the stumps; heavy flies for deep water and less-weighted ones for shallow water.

In deadfalls at least 3 or more feet deep, fish weedless flies. Let them tumble into the branches, then lift the rod tip. Fish the deeper parts of logjams in the same manner.

Boat docks have lots of good places for the vertical drop; in fact, the edges of floating docks are ideal for the presentation. Cast the fly onto the dock's floor, then pull it off gently to let it drop into the water. Spinners, twister tails, and flies with rubber hackles are the ideal candidates. Dock supports and the shaded areas beneath elevated docks are good targets, too. The vertical drop is the best presentation for fish-cleaning stations. Use light-colored flies that include white, silver, and red materials.

Fish the edges of soft-stemmed vegetation with Woolly Buggers, W.I.T.H. Buggers, and worm and snake imitations. Fish tight to the face of the weeds and make contact if the plants are forgiving enough. If the fly hangs up, strip it free and continue the drop.

The vertical drop is the most logical way to present flies to an ambush predator, and more large bass are caught when it's utilized. Consider the possibilities on all the waters you fish and your catches will likely improve.

Chapter 6

Fishing the Mid-Depths

Where shallow water ends and deep water begins is arbitrary at best. We can define "shallow" as the area where bass can see, or in muddy water sense, well enough to respond to a surface fly or floater/diver. If "deep" depends on the same criteria in relation to the bottom, then mid-depth could conceivably be between 2 feet and more than 60 feet. That's unwieldy. So understanding the wide parameters we might need to define mid-depth, its fly-fishing tactics are most frequently and practically applied between 3 and 8 feet.

Mid-depth fly-fishing can be most difficult simply because we can neither see our flies nor feel the bottom. It's important, again, that we accurately determine the desired depth. In this respect, we depend on the countdown discussed in the previous chapter, but we also remember imparting action to the fly moves it toward the surface. Depending on the speed and duration of the strip we use, an abbreviated count between strips is needed to allow the fly to return to the desired depth. Each time we manipulate the fly, the process must be repeated until it's picked up and recast.

Practically speaking, floating line becomes a hindrance beyond a depth of about 4 feet. While there are exceptions, our terminal tackle for mid-depth fishing includes floating line with leaders of 6 to 9 feet, and sink-tip or full-sinking line with 3 1/2- to 7 1/2-foot leaders. All vertical drop flies are effective at mid-depth. Generally, flies that quickly reach the depth we believe will be productive and are reasonably easy to keep there will be effective. Some patterns can be adapted more readily than others.

The ideal rod for mid-depth fishing handles both floating and sinking lines well. In the uppermost layer of mid-depth, 4 to 5 feet from the surface, it's possible to cast floating line using 9-foot leaders. Tippet strength must be matched to the targeted cover, but should also be the lightest possible for the weight and size of the selected flies. When fishing the 6- to 8-feet deep portions of mid-depth a sinking line with a 4- to 6-foot leader perform best.

Most of us are quite visually oriented. We might be comfortable fishing a piece of cover attached to the shoreline, but feel completely out of synch without a visible casting target. Our introduction to this concept and the importance of probing the mid-depths was a complete accident.

Years ago, we were using our trolling motor to stay within casting range of a brushy bank when a gust of wind pushed us off course. Our flies trailed off the stern of the boat as we glided back into position. Suddenly, one rod was nearly jerked away. A bass skittered across the surface before it was subdued and released. We had drifted at least 40 feet from our shallow target, but didn't grasp the significance of the catch until the accident was repeated 30 minutes later. Locator reconnaissance revealed that the estuary, formed by the creek that entered the lake at the back of the cove, formed a horseshoe bend with a brushy saddle between its bends. Our two accidental drifts had produced two nice bass from structure we didn't even know existed. Fly-fishermen often concede these bountiful areas to spin-fishermen. This particular bass hotspot, while 40 feet from the nearest shore, had brush tops extending within 6 feet of the surface with creek channel depths of 14 feet on either side. We've only seen other boats on the location twice. Both times they were fishing for crappies that used the saddle seasonally as a holding area before the spawn.

Largemouth bass spend most of their time associated with members of their own clan. We call these groupings schools, although the number of fish in them varies greatly from a few to several dozen. During the spawn they remove themselves from the school and respond to their individual urges, but after males scatter the last of the fry, most rejoin their contemporaries in the school until the next spawn. Just as in the human population, however, there are those that are solitary throughout the year. As anglers we need to determine whether we should try to tempt solitary maverick bass or locate the school. Both can be challenging tasks. There are times when either is a good approach, but philosophically, at least, fishing success is most consistent when we find a school. Bait-casters have long embraced the "find the school" concept, and fly-casters can be equally successful with it.

There are six situations that call for mid-depth tactics: suspended bass, points, inlet creeks, fishing "the walls," logjams, and tickling the tops of structure. In each location, we can present flies by stationary casting, trolling, or controlled-drifting. We have chosen, therefore, to address our recommendations for specific mid-depth flies and retrieves for mid-depth fishing as we encounter them.

Suspended Bass

Largemouth bass suspend more frequently in summer and winter than in spring or fall. Warmer water in winter or cooler water in summer and protection from sunlight could be the reasons. They can also suspend near a food source, such as a school of shad. Locating suspended bass can be difficult. Anglers can find suspended bass by randomly scouring the lake with a locator, but instances of seeing fish with the locator, then catching them, are relatively rare in our experience. Recognizing the extent of sunlight penetration into the water is an important observation. Taking the water temperature at various depths helps in finding them, too.

If casting to the usual shore-bound cover and checking out the other mid-depth locations proves fruitless, there's a good chance that much of the bass population is suspended. Keeping sunlight and water temperature in mind, there are three prime locations that could lead to discovery of those suspended bass. Look for them over creek channels, in the mouths of coves, and in standing timber.

Reservoir creek channels serve as highways for bass schools. You can bet there are some along their lengths much of the time. If you can find a bend in a channel with appropriate depth to reduce sunlight penetration and moderate water temperature, it's worth fishing carefully. Any successful spots should be noted so you can return to the location on subsequent trips. The previously discussed accidental encounter with bass on the brushy saddle illustrates the importance of looking for suspended bass along submerged creek channels.

Fan cast the area from an anchored boat, but if it's breezy this can be difficult in open water. Trolling or controlled drifting can be much more effective. To troll an area, you must have your fly at the right depth while keeping one eye on the locator to stay on the structure, and the other eye on your path of travel while paying attention to the slightest bump. Make no mistake, fishing in this manner can make you busier than a one-eyed dog in a butcher shop. It can also be the key to finding the mother lode.

Controlled drifting differs from trolling because the angler uses the wind to push his craft along the structure and activates the motor only when it's necessary to alter his path. If the breeze is cooperative, it's a bit easier to perform.

On a recent autumn afternoon, we began searching for bass. Just two weeks earlier, we had exciting action in the backs of coves when 12- to 15-inch fish were chasing schools of shad, but air temperature had plummeted to an unseasonably cool 28 degrees the night before. As the front passed through, it left a blue-sky afternoon of 60 degrees. It was obvious jump-fishing the shad bursts was history, so we checked a couple of secondary points and a main-lake point without success. Finally, we wised up and turned on the locator. An old river channel brushed the edge of a main lake point and ran down a long bluff. On the inside of the former river's edge were clusters of fish we felt certain were largemouths. They were tightly gathered in depressions near brush. They were also in a negative feeding mood and we couldn't move them. They hadn't migrated far from where we had expected to find them, but had simply backed off the point to ride out the cold front.

Bass frequently suspend in the mouths of coves—the narrower the passage, the better. Secondary cove mouths can be as productive as those on the main lake. Bass in these locations might relate to the points or use the area as a rest stop in their travels. The cove's slender passages offer comfort and safety and tend to tightly bunch passing baitfish so they can be easily ambushed. Try the Cowen's Coyote discussed in Chapter 5 for suspended bass. It has the heft to get down fast, and, after the strip, it drops back to the desired depth quickly. It's a versatile fly that can be used in lots of different situations, and its effectiveness on the horizontal strip makes it perform particularly well with suspended bass. Clousers, an old standby for suspended bass, can be tied using smaller barbell eyes so they can be retrieved slowly.

There's so much standing timber in our home lakes going from tree to tree just isn't feasible. We look for the best ones along the bends in creek channels, on humps or other irregular breaks. Bass suspend in tree branches, for example, (Diagram 6-A) if the branches are located at 15 feet deep and the bottom at 30 feet. They can also be located facing tree trunks all the way to their bases (Diagram 6-B). Generally, if bass are high in the tree they're active and catchable. If they're located facing the trunks and deep they're not worth the time.

Diagram 6-A

Diagram 6-B

In summer, standing timber is a good place to look for cold-front fish, but they're tough to catch. Standing timber also holds late fall and winter bass. Again, you can easily read their attitude by their position on the tree. On sunny days they tend to be higher in the treetops, where they're probably in search of the slightly warmer water. Usually, a few degrees of warmth make them more active and they'll take advantage of the opportunity to feed. These feeders should be pursued, but don't expect them to chase your fly as they might in the spring. They'll wait for flies to come close to their positions even if they've previously seen your presentation from several feet away. We've seldom experienced fast fishing under these conditions, although larger fish seem to be the rule. This situation presents an excellent opportunity to land the season's biggest bass. In spite of that, we know it can be frustrating. At times, the extended limbs seem to grab every effort to entice a fish. That momentary hesitation caused by limb contact brings about some solid hook-sets and firmly attached flies. Trying to free the fly and eventually breaking off can be frustrating by itself, and fish in that treetop will become tight-lipped from the commotion. Locating another productive tree isn't as easy as it sounds. Use your locator in treetops near creek channels, on humps or submerged points.

Cowen's Flap Tail Shad is the perfect fly for working late-season treetops. Drop slack line into the water and allow the fly to drop vertically to a position in the treetop immediately beneath you. When it's fallen to the desired depth, lift the rod tip slowly then let the fly fall again. The colder the water, the more times this yo-yoing process might need to be repeated.

Points

Points of land that continue as submerged bars into progressively deeper water can be excellent mid-depth bass attractors. Look for immediate access to deep water and some cover, such as weeds or brush. Sunlight penetration and water temperature indicate where, along the point, bass might be located. Clousers work well on points, as do crayfish imitations if the point's composition is gravel or chunk rock. A good mid-depth pattern for fishing points is the W.I.T.H. Bugger created by Lake Fork, Texas guide Rob Woodruff. The name is an acronym for "What In The Hell," and the movement of its many tentacles attracts big bass. Woodruff says the top three colors for him have been brown/blue, and black/red, and olive/black, although he ties it in 18 color combinations.

Rob's W.I.T.H. Bugger (brown/blue)

Hook: Mustad 3366 2/0
Head: 3/16-inch Wapsi Cyclops Eye
Thread: Brown Danville Flat Waxed
  Nylon
Weed Guard: 30-lb. Mason Hard
  Mono
Legs: 9 pumpkin/blue tipped Wapsi
  Sili Legs or other silicone leg
  material
Body: One 10-inch piece brown
  medium chenille and one 10-inch
  piece blue tinsel chenille
Hackle: Brown rooster saddle
Tail: Brown marabou

Rob's W.I.T.H. Bugger is deadly along weed banks and over carpets of vegetation.

Mash down hook barb and slide bead up to eye of hook. Melt a ball on one end of a 4 1/2-inch piece of hard mono. Tie in the ball end of the mono on top of the hook just above the hook point, and secure it at the hook bend.

Tie in a clump of marabou approximately the length of hook shank above the hook point. Tie in Sili Legs in front of the tail clump and arrange them around the hook shank. The legs should extend back slightly past the end of the marabou. Pull the longer end of the Sili Legs up to the bead and wrap the thread forward to the bead.

On left side of the hook shank, tie in tinsel chenille just behind the bead at the hook eye and lash them back to the tail clump. Bring the thread back up to the bead. On the right side of the hook shank, tie in standard chenille just behind the bead. Wrap the thread back to the tail clump. Wrap the chenille back to the tail and tie it down to create a smooth underbody. Tie an overhand knot on top of the hook shank with 2 pieces of chenille, then tie an overhand knot under the hook shank.

Tie in the saddle hackle in front of the chenille knots. Tie overhand knots alternating over and under the hook shank all the way to the bead, making sure the standard chenille is the top piece in the knot. Palmer hackle forward to the bead.

Flatten the last 1/8 inch of mono weed guard and slip it through the hole in the bead under the hook shank. Pull the end of the mono past the hook eye until the desired curve in the weed guard is reached. Clip off the excess mono and melt a ball on the end that's too large to pass back through the hole in the bead. Pull the weed guard backwards so the ball rests against the front of the bead. Pull the front set of legs forward, make several wraps behind them, and 2 half-hitches. Pull legs backward and whip finish between the front of the legs and the back of the bead. Trim the front and rear sets of legs just past the marabou.

Tail-spinner flies are another good choice for probing points. The Thunder-Spin and the Flap Tail Shad are two examples. They take a bit more patience for their natural vertical drop, but remember to watch for a telltale bump or hesitation. Most point strikes occur either on the initial drop or as the fly resettles after the strip.

The most effective retrieve for points involves casting toward the shallow end of the point, then hopping the fly into progressively deeper water. The top of the point can be most productive, but its sides also descend into deep water. Although our description of points seems to apply to big reservoirs, we often fished a pond of less than 5 acres with three points that were prime bass locations. In small water, the deeper sides of points are usually superior.

Points are one of the best bass locations on any water. On large reservoirs, they receive lots of attention from bait- and spin-fishermen, but on small waters they're seldom the focus of attention. As a result, the resident bass population isn't acquainted with a constant barrage of phony food and they tend to be more catchable.

Trolling or controlled drifting across points at an appropriate depth can provide a pattern for consistent action. We haven't yet equipped our float tubes with locators, but we know other fly-fishers who have. We troll and employ a controlled drift in our tubes when we fish points in small water. A good fly for working points is the Cowen's E-Z Body

Rattler first conceived by Georgia guide Henry Cowen. It's a baitfish pattern with action and sound.

Cowen's E-Z Body Rattler
Hook: Mustad 34007, size 2/0
Head: E-Z Body tubing with epoxy
Body: Crosscut rabbit strip white
Back: 10 to 12 strands of peacock herl over chartreuse polar fiber over several strands of pearl Flashabou
Tail: White Zonker strip impaled on a 30-pound mono spike tied to extend from the bend 3/8 inch. Burn the mono end to prevent the Zonker strip from wrapping on the hook
Eyes: Small silver prismatic stick-on

Inlet Creeks

Largemouth bass locate at inflows for food and warmer water in spring and cooler water in summer. Largemouths won't be found in current, but they position themselves near slow eddies to let food wash to them. Eddies have crosscurrents that make fishing there tough. A still surface can belie moving water beneath that carries flies into submerged rootwads. Cast into the current and let the fly drift into still water before imparting action that brings the fly toward the rod tip. Slack line is difficult to control in current, and missed strikes are common. Mid-depth flies for the mouths of inlet creeks are baitfish imitations, Woolly Buggers, Batmans (recipe in Chapter 7), Cowen's Coyotes, Squirrel Spins, Clousers, and E-Z Deceivers (recipe in Chapter 7).

Fishing the "Walls"

Another outstanding bass location is structure we call "the wall." We look for four types of walls: bluffs, weedlines, downed timber, and docks. All can provide the shade and cover to hold lots of bass.

Bluffs, depending on their location, can be shaded when other areas of the lake are exposed to full sun. Many were created when a creek channel spent eons cutting into its banks. Small waters can have bluffs. The prime location on natural bluffs is the downstream side where a creek channel butted against the bluff, then flowed away. The upstream end can hold bass as well, but the downstream ledge is much better. If there's a series of ledges that stair-step toward the bottom, they can be very productive. Cast to points and pockets along the bluff's length, too.

An occasional cast away from the bluff isn't a bad tactic, either. As the creek meandered along the bluff it probably created a shallower side on the inside bend. It could be a very good location, particularly if there is other structure present.

Clousers, Bass Bullys, tail-spinners, and leech patterns can be productive, and one of our favorite tactics here is using baitfish imitations on full-sinking lines. Boulder Junction, Wisconsin, fly shop owner and guide, Bill Sherer, ties a fly that's dynamite for this location. The B. P. Muskie Fly is big, measuring 7 to 10 inches, and it features a lip, which enables the fly-rodder to fish it as a bait-caster would a crank bait. Experience with this soft closed-cell foam fly tied originally for muskies can get you to depths of 6 feet. Here's Bill's recipe:

B.P. Muskie Fly

Hook: Mustad custom-made 6XL Kink-shank, extra heavy wire, triple chrome plated 5/0, or 2/0 - 902233S; Tiemco 511S 2/0

Thread: White Gudebrod "G"

Diving Lip: 10 mil die cut Mylar

Undertail: Yellow over orange marabou

Tail: 4 olive saddle hackles 6 to 8 inches long

Overtail: Olive marabou with olive rainbow thread on sides

Head: 3/8-inch X 3/8-inch X 3-inch Evazote foam tied in after diving lip and colored with waterproof art markers

Eyes: 7mm posted red plastic eyes super glued into sockets in head

Form the Diving Lip: Lay pre-cut Mylar on a 90-degree table edge, and pinch to make a crease that will form a trough down its center from the narrow end to 1 inch from the wide end. While holding the creased part together, fold down the remaining inch. Attach thread behind the kink in the hook shank. Place the lip's trough under the hook shank so that the downturned portion is just behind the hook eye, and tightly overwrap while pinching the Mylar trough together. Take care to keep the lip perpendicular to the hook eye so the fly will track straight and upright when it's retrieved. When the downturned lip begins to turn just past 90 degrees as the wraps advance nearer the hook eye, run the thread directly onto the hook shank. Wrap to the hook eye and make two half hitches.

Body and Tail: Center the foam strip across the hook shank just behind the hook eye, make two figure-eight wraps over the foam and hook shank, two wraps of thread around the foam parachute post style, then two reverse wraps around the hook shank in front of the foam. Make two half hitches behind the foam and continue the thread to the rear by wrapping tightly to completely cover the Mylar. The Mylar should be firmly seated against the hook shank sides around the kink. Tie in saddle hackles on top of the hook shank, attach marabou to the top of the saddles, and add Krystal Flash to each side of the hook shank. Pull the ends of the foam back and tie them to the top of the hook shank on top of the tail wraps. Whip finish, and trim the foam ends.

   Bend the lip forward, crease each corner, and trim about 1/8 inch off each. Color the foam with waterproof markers, dark over light. Glue on eyes.

Note: To tune the lip, keep in mind a flattened lip will wiggle tightly but stay near the surface. A tightly pinched lip will wiggle less, but dive deeper.

   Whitlock's Match the Minnow flies are good when fishing bluffs. On big water, shad imitators are an obvious choice, too, but don't overlook a pattern that imitates little bluegills.

   Some ponds have bluffs constructed of mud or clay. Alone, they're little used by the largemouth population, so look for something that enhances their attractiveness. If they're exposed to frequent wind and wave action, an undercut bank usually results. It can serve as shady overhead protection and could be an important location. Erosion can cause soil and brush or small trees to tumble down the embankment to create suitable structure. There are rarely inundated creek channels in ponds, but there could still be a shelf or two created if part of the bluff's face fell into the water during a heavy downpour. If the bluff provides

Chapter 4
Shallow-Water Flies

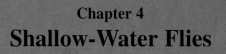

Verduin's Ball-Joint Popper, page 72
Tied by Michael Verduin

Dahlberg Diver (Original), page 73
Tied by John Henry

Dahlberg Fur-Strip Diver, page 74
Tied by John Henry

Mega-Diver, page 74
Tied by John Henry

Wiggle Minnow, page 75
Tied by Bill Sherer

Chapter 4
Shallow-Water Flies

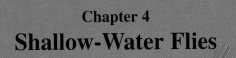

Ginger Woollie, page 79
Tied by Terry Wilson

Wilson's Jointed Sally, page 80
Tied by Terry Wilson

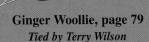

Cowen's Coyote, page 82
Tied by Henry Cowen

Chapter 5
Vertical-Drop Flies

Wilson's Bass Bully, page 91
Tied by Terry Wilson

Rabbit Strip Leech (Fur Leech), page 91
Tied by John Henry

Chapter 5
Vertical-Drop Flies

Squirrel Spin, page 93
Tied by Terry Wilson

Thunder-Spin, page 92
Tied by Terry Wilson

Flap Tail Shad, page 93
Tied by Henry Cowen

Calcasieu Pig Boat (modified), page 94
Tied by Tom Nixon

Whitlock's Eelworm Streamer, page 96
Tied by John Henry

Whitlock's Hare Worm, page 96
Tied by John Henry

Chapter 6
Mid-Depth Flies

Rob's W.I.T.H. Bugger, page 108
Tied by Rob Woodruff

Cowen's E-Z Body Rattler, page 110
Tied by Henry Cowen

B.P. Muskie Fly, page 111
Tied by Bill Sherer

BUBfly, page 114
Tied by Chuck Tryon

Woodruff's Swamp Rabbit, page 114
Tied by Rob Woodruff

Baggie Bendback, page 116
Tied by Bill Sherer

Chapter 7
Deep-Water Flies

Batman, page 125
Tied by Kevin Cohenour

Lead-Eyed Bunny Booger, page 126
Tied by John Henry

Wilson's Rattle Snake, page 127
Tied by Terry Wilson

Tanner's Clouser Minnow, page 128
Tied by Terry Tanner

E-Z Deceiver, page 131
Tied by Terry Wilson

1. Evening is the magic time of poppers and summer bucketmouths.

2. Largemouths are ambushed predators with compact bodies capable of thrashing and sometimes acrobatic fights.

3. Any fish capable of doubling a nine-weight rod requires specialized gear.

4. Aggressive surface strikes and explosive leaps have hooked generations of fly-casters.

5. Float tubes offer comfortable access to areas that are out of reach for most anglers.

1.

2.

3.

1. Inlet creeks can either warm or cool still-water while providing oxygen and food.

2. Traditional cork poppers still fool lots of big bass.

3. Warmwater discharge lakes offer year-round largemouth fly fishing.

shade when the surrounding shallow structure is sunlit, it can serve as a temporary bass shelter. Mud or clay can also cause water at the bluff's base to be cloudy from suspended silt, and the silty layer can shield bass from direct sunlight. Especially in small waters, these dirt and clay bluffs deserve attention.

Weedlines

Solid weedlines, such as those composed of milfoil, duckweed, or coontail, can be fished similarly to bluffs. Instead of locating on ledges, bass simply find a hole in the weeds where they can face open water. Fishing parallel to the "wall" of weeds can provide the angler with lots of information about where fish are located. They'll likely be higher in the weedline than on an equivalent rock bluff. The reason is weeds tend to cool the water while rocks reflect the sun and make it warmer.

If the weedline isn't very deep, fishing parallel to it can spook more fish than it warrants. How close the angler can approach without alarming fish is a decision that must constantly be reevaluated. Baitfish imitations can be good along weed banks, but so are rabbit strip leeches with weed guards. They tumble enticingly down the wall, occasionally hanging up before continuing their descent.

Rob's W.I.T.H. Bugger is an excellent pattern for weedlines. The movement of its tentacles as it drops through the water column enables the fly to attract attention without forcing the angler to strip it away from his target. Don't forget that veggie-bumping with Clousers and Woolly Buggers is effective here, too.

In smaller waters, clumps of cattails, water willows, or other woody vegetation offer bass cover and food. Flies cast into them are guaranteed goners, but the outside edges present a situation that's good for wall presentations. Woolly Buggers, weighted or unweighted, with Krystal Flash added to their marabou tails, and variations that incorporate rubber hackles are excellent choices. One such variation, Chuck Tryon's BUBfly (BUB is an acronym for Big Ugly Bug), has rubber hackles at both ends for attractive action. He dubbed his yellow version a Banana BUB, and it's one of our favorites for farm pond and river bass. A fishing pal swears by purple BUBflies after he landed a 19 1/2-inch largemouth from a deep hole beside a huge rootwad in one of our Ozark rivers.

BUBfly (yellow)

Hook: Mustad 9674 or 9672 down-eye, size 6
Thread: Yellow 6/0
Underbody: .030 lead wire or chenille
Overbody: Yellow chenille, extra fine or medium
Hackle: Palmered rooster saddle hackle solid or dyed grizzly hackle
Tails and Antennae: Medium square yellow rubber hackle
Note: A bead head or bead-chain eyes may be added. For the palmered hackle, he recommends stiff ones for moving water and lower-grade hackles for still water. We tie BUBflies in white, yellow, black, or purple. Light colors are good in spring and fall; dark ones are better in summer.

Docks

Manmade docks provide another wall opportunity. To be consistent producers, docks must have immediate access to deep water. Additional cover of any kind enhances their attractiveness to bass. Look for docks with fish-cleaning stations on them. If the stations are used with any regularity bass take up residence underneath to let the dock owner provide a regular buffet for them.

One fly that's hard to beat when it's fished around the edges of docks is the Woodruff's Swamp Rabbit. It utilizes a vinyl twister tail for action on the drop and undulates seductively on the retrieve. This bulky pattern also incorporates sound in the form of rattles. Rattles are effective if they're worked with a jerking action.

Woodruff's Swamp Rabbit (black/red)

Hook: Mustad 3366 or 3366B, size 2/0
Thread: Black Danville Flat Waxed Nylon, or color to match front fur strip
Weed Guard: Mason Hard Mono
Tail: Half of a Stanley Jig's Pro Trailer with rattle unit, or a large Wapsi Fly Tail

Rattle: Wapsi Fly Rattle, or small Venom glass rattle
Eyes: 1/36-ounce lead dumbbell eyes and red hologram eyes with black
   pupils
Body: Black rabbit fur strips and red rabbit fur strip
Head: Built-up thread coated with 5-minute epoxy or head cement

When fishing off docks, other effective flies include the Bass Bully, the B. P. Muskie Fly, and any baitfish or leech imitation. Casting position and accuracy are important considerations here. Casts that are made progressively shallower spook far fewer fish. Unless we have good reason to believe the bass are shallow, as they are during the spawn, our first casts are made along the outside edge of the dock. If there's anchored trees or brush just off the edge, the outside edge is a good starting point. The next casts are placed into empty boat stalls. Fish the backs and inside edges carefully and slowly. Vertical-drop flies are excellent here, because any bass positioned nearby listen and watch for an easy meal. If there's a walkway that leads to the dock, the corner warrants exploration.

Deadfalls

Downed timber at the water's edge, especially a fallen tree with branches extending into deep water can present a wooded wall. Fish deeper branches first, then work progressively shallower. This prevents accidental splashdowns and hang-ups from spooking bass along the entire length of the tree. Don't be afraid to throw weedless offerings right into the densest cover. Allow the fly to fall between the branches. As the offering drops from limb to limb, lift the rod tip and make a short strip before allowing the fly to fall again. In this situation, it's not advisable to set the hook with each line hesitation, but experience soon enables the angler to recognize the difference between branches and hungry bass.

An excellent fly for this situation is a unique weedless streamer created, again, by Bill Sherer. The Baggie Bendback is a clever version of the weedless fly, and we like it in very large, 1/0 to 4/0, sizes. It makes a sputtering sound as it's cast, but it snakes over and through branches like no other. It's a weedless pattern that fishes well anyplace minnows and tough cover meet.

Baggie Bendback

Hook: Mustad 34011 #10 (4/0 bent down to form bendback style)
Thread: Black 3/0
Body: Pearl Diamond Braid
Underwing: Saltwater Krystal Flash & 2 grizzly saddle hackles
Wing: 2 mil plastic bag cut to minnow shape
Overwing: Bucktail & 6 strands of Olive Rainbow Thread
Eyes: 5/32-inch hologram
Head: E-Z Shape Sparkle Body Pearl

Logjams

Most large impoundments have logjams, places where winds have mashed sticks, logs, and blow-downs into a confined area. They could be piled against bluffs or in small coves off the main lake. Lots of anglers pass them up because they have a foreboding appearance that suggests no lure or fly could survive a trip through them. Most flies land on exposed wood, and must be coaxed into crevices or pocket openings. Short, accurate casts are necessary, as is the patience to crawl flies into holes so the offerings drop vertically into position. Strip, and release the line allowing the fly to move up and down into the bass's vision several times. If the bass hits in this situation the odds are decidedly in his favor, but rest assured it's a great presentation.

For logjams, use very heavy tippets and check them often. When they feel rough as you run your fingers along them, change tippets to prevent breakoffs. Weedless leech patterns, Calcasieu Pig Boats, and Baggie Bendbacks are good in logjams, too.

Tickling the Tops Of Structure

The final mid-depth approach is tickling the tops of weeds or brush. Any type of weed growth that emerges from the bottom and grows toward, but hasn't reached, the surface is a good contender for this tactic. Flies with enough weight to fall to the tops of the weeds and cause some disturbance, but not break through the roof of the vegetation, are just right. Cowen's Coyotes, Rob's W.I.T.H. Buggers, Batmans (recipe in Chapter 7), and Baggie Bendbacks all do the job. This roof-shaking presentation is best when the fare is crawled along with periodic lifts of the rod tip that cause the fly to flutter toward the surface, then drop back to the weeds or brush tops. It could be the commotion is annoying or threatening to the bass, and their objective is to kill the disturbance-causing varmint rather than feed.

In the late 1980s we occasionally fished Kentucky Lake. It was edged in milfoil that by late summer reached the surface from depths of 20 feet. On several occasions we fished with resort owner Butch McElwain, who wielded a 9 1/2-foot 9-weight rod with power and finesse. Even in the heat of July midday he fished a popper or a floater-diver. He cast to the edges of open pockets and intentionally snagged the milfoil. The purpose was aggressively freeing the fly and walking it across the matted roof of weeds into the pockets. It was a tactic that made the bass jittery. Frequently, a bass charged the imitation with so much ferocity that the milfoil salad was sprayed in all directions. Those strikes were as spectacular as any we've witnessed, and 20- to 21-inch largemouths were not uncommon. It was an impressive demonstration of "veggie-bumping."

There are several flies that work well over submerged brush. Minnow imitations are good, as are Woolly Buggers, E-Z Deceivers (recipe in Chapter 7), and marabou streamers. Strip-and-pause retrieves are productive, but be prepared to sacrifice some flies.

Tickling the tops of weeds, as with all mid-depth locations except logjams, is an excellent place to utilize trolling or controlled drifting.

For a few years we had access to a private bass pond that was carefully monitored. The small water received lots of pressure from fishers who came long distances to accept the warm hospitality of the owner. Many walked the pond's banks and tossed their wares along the edges of the weedbeds. Some used a small pram and a canoe paddle that were always left along the bank, but they, too, always cast toward the weedline. We spent our time throwing and mid-depth flies along a line of uncut brush and a small tree line just out of the other anglers' casting range. We often had greater success than the weedline fishers because the population of bass that either resided in, or migrated to, the mid-depth brush and timber saw only our flies rather than a constant barrage.

Targeting Structure At Mid-Depth

There are several other types of structure that can be fished at mid-depth successfully, but keep in mind all targets must be in 4 to 8 feet of water.

Dams and spillways are great places for heavily weighted crayfish patterns. If these are places that are 4 to 5 feet deep, you can get by with floating lines and 9-foot leaders. If the places are deeper, sinking lines are required. The difference is floating line forces the fly toward the rod tip on the strip. This can be a good retrieve, but if it's not productive and you feel the fish are there, don't hesitate to switch to short, 4-foot leaders and full-sinking lines. If there are other structural elements in evidence, such as deadfalls or weeds, it's a great place to match the minnow. Streamers that imitate small bluegills, crappies, or perch are effective. Count down the fly to the tops of weeds or deadfall and impart short, quick strips interspersed with pauses to simulate the naturals. Generally, you might want to start facing riprap so the fly can be worked deeper or shallower until you connect. Fan cast if the focus area is an irregular feature, but drift or controlled drift if the dam's riprap is uniform.

Bottom composition changes that are located in water 4 to 8 feet deep can be fished with baitfish imitations, natural-colored leeches or big, dark-colored flies, such as Woolly Buggers, E-Z Deceivers (Chapter 7) and other jig-type flies. Count them down and strip them back to simulate an undulating motion.

If there's vegetation on the crest of a hump, it's almost certainly a gathering place for baitfish. Weighted streamers that imitate small sunfish can be exceptional there. They should be stripped with quick, darting, 2-inch strips and an erratic change-of-direction retrieve. If the hump is composed of rocks, a heavily weighted crayfish imitation could be the ticket to success. If there is a significant hump, explore it with a locator periodically to see if fish use it. Largemouths use steep humps as transitional locations, during pre-spawn and pre-summer.

Islands, as mid-depth fishing locations, are fished the same as humps. They simply offer more options. If the island has an attached ridge it should be explored, but if there's no additional cover bass might only use it as a transitional location.

Look for creek channels in the appropriate depth with sharp turns and additional cover. Creek channels with both can be the best summertime big bass magnets in the lake. If you can see the fish on the locator, it can be most productive to stationary cast the specific area using baitfish imitations over the shallower structure and a heavy headed jig-type fly in the deeper areas. If the creek channel twists and turns for a considerable distance, but remains between 4 and 8 feet deep, try trolling or a controlled drift using weighted streamers.

Undercut banks are good mid-depth targets. Sidearm cast streamers or bulky flies with rubber hackles or rabbit strips, allow them to sink, and strip them slowly to achieve an undulating motion.

Mid-depth stumps can best be fished with a heavy-headed jig-type fly and the change-of-direction or stump-bumping techniques. Also, slowly strip spinner flies and sunfish imitations past the stumps' shady sides. A strip and pause creates an erratic tracking pattern that a big bass could intercept. A Wilson's Jointed Sally crawled slowly along a stump's base could prompt an attack.

Our experiences have validated for us the importance of fishing efficiently in the mid-depths of all our waters. It's an area that should not be conceded to the spin-fishing population. A fly-fisherman's tools are quite appropriate for fishing mid-depths and they offer the advantages of a stealthy delivery and more pliable materials that move through the bass's world far more naturally than any hardware.

Going Deep

Although shallow water has traditionally been the bailiwick of the largemouth fly-fisher, the mid-depth area is near enough to at least draw consideration. Deep water, on the other hand, is foreign territory. This is understandable, at least in the respect that the sinking lines that make deep fly-fishing possible are a relatively new concept. It's not only possible to fish deep water efficiently; it can be a very enjoyable and rewarding experience as well.

Again, some definition is necessary. "Deep" can be the most relative term to describe location that a fisherman can use. If we relate it only to the bottom and flies that are fished in contact with the bottom, it falls short of reasonable. That's why we included some bottom contact fishing in discussing the shallows (i.e., salamanders in spawning areas, Chapter 4) and mid-depths (i.e., crayfish and tail-spinner flies fished on points, Chapter 6). The bottom must be part of any definition of deep fishing. If not, by our definition, the situation would rightly belong in the mid-depth category. Deep is also relative to the depth of the water discussed. Big, steep-sided reservoirs, often found in hilly country, with maximum depths over a hundred feet surely require 10 to 20 feet of water to even begin referring to deep water. A sprawling backwater lake found along a major river system can have a maximum depth of 7 feet with wide expanses of mud flats that are only 2 to 3 feet under water. There, we might start talking about 5 feet as deep.

We must recognize if the bottom we want to fish is 20 feet deep and we make a 30-foot cast to allow the weighted fly and sinking line to make contact with the bottom, the fly stops its descent almost directly beneath our position. When we begin to manipulate the fly it has a very short distance to bounce or flutter before it's stripped upward toward the rod tip. The tactic becomes a vertical jigging or yo-yoing process very quickly. Conventional casting requires throwing more line, which enables the fly to spend more time near the bottom. Yet maximum depths must be reasonable. For us the limit is 20 feet.

Lake Fork, Texas, guide Rob Woodruff agrees. He points out two facts that must be considered when fishing deep water.

First, the length of time for full-sinking 6-rated line to reach a depth of 20 feet, "depending on the weight and resistance of the fly, requires forty-six seconds." That's about the maximum amount of time we're willing to wait before imparting action.

Second, Rob points out, making a positive hook-set can be difficult. "If someone held a size-2/0 hook with the line attached to a bait-casting rod 50 feet away, the hook couldn't be pulled from the holder's grip." Add to that the problem of strike detection at increased distances and our self-imposed 20-foot depth limit is understandable.

Twenty feet of depth can be fished efficiently with a fly rod. Fifty- to sixty-foot casts are necessary, and we need to guess the point the fly contacts the bottom so we can cast beyond the area we want to fish. This enables a retrieve of reasonable length in productive water. The definition, then, of deep fly-fishing, while arbitrary, is presenting a fly that's in contact with the bottom for at least part of the retrieve in water at least 5 feet deep but no more than 20 feet deep. Fly-fishers are capable of fishing deeper, it's just that it becomes a vertical jigging operation and the fun of casting is lost.

Deep water requires rods capable of relatively long casts with full-sinking lines and enough backbone to execute a vigorous hook-set.

Diagram 7

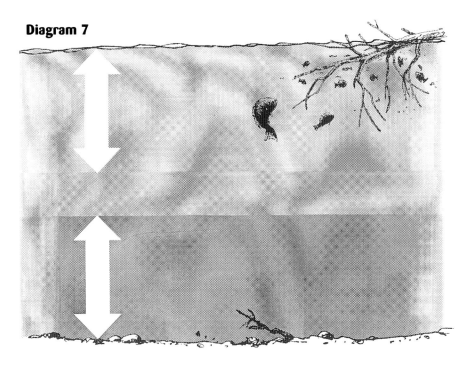

Leaders of 4 to 6 feet need to have tippet strengths of 16- to 20-pound test to accommodate the extra heavy flies normally used here.

The primary reason for removing extreme depths from the equation is during the summer still waters stratify into three distinct layers distinguished by their temperature. The colder, heavier water near the bottom is known as the hypolimnion. This layer becomes oxygen-depleted and is therefore uninhabitable by fish. The warmer upper layer near the surface, or epilimnion, is home to the piscatorial population. There is a relatively narrow band of water known as the thermocline, which is a transitional area between the upper fish zone and the lower no-fish zone. The thermocline acts as a glass bottom that might as well be the fishing lake bottom. The situation is caused by temperature, but oxygen determines where fish live.

Anglers can easily discover where the thermocline is located in their waters by checking water temperatures at descending depths. For our purpose, then, the thermocline is the point at which the temperature begins to drop rapidly (Diagram 7). This transitional layer continues until the layer of essentially uniform temperature (hypolimnion).

As the surface temperature drops in autumn, lakes reach the point where the surface is cooler than the bottom. The cooler, heavier water on the bottom rises to the top where oxygen is replenished. When this happens, we say the lake has turned over. In the winter, when there is no thermocline and the water is oxygenated from top to bottom, bass can be scattered at a wide range of depths. The range can include very deep water.

One of the reservoirs we regularly fish has a long, steep-sided point that extends into the depths of the main lake. It's made of clay and gravel with lots of football- to Volkswagen-sized rocks but supports little vegetation. The location gets a lot of attention from other anglers, but usually there are some 12- to 15-inch bass from shallow to 20 feet deep. Boats can be positioned in the shallows for casts into deep water. Anglers can hop the fly toward the rod, cast from deep to shallow, or cast across the point from either side. Flies with enough heft to kick up silt clouds and make audible sounds when stripped into the rocks can be fished successfully there. It's a location many fly-casters can overlook, but it's the very definition of deep water. However this point is fished, from whichever direction, bottom contact must be made for part of the retrieve.

Deep-water hook-sets must be powerful. Difficulty in strike detection increases in direct relation to its distance from the rod tip. Consider the length of time in transmitting the strike's signal to the faraway angler. The chances of the fly's rejection before the angler reacts to it increase with distance. Also consider the problem of overcoming the stretch of the line and leader, as well as the flex in the rod before hook penetration occurs. All of these conditions recommend a truly vigorous hook-set in deep water.

Random casting over deep bottom is not a good idea. Too much lake bottom is devoid of bass-holding structure and simply a waste of time. (Deep, slow pools in rivers are another matter, because they can hold the biggest fish.) All lake or pond bottoms consist of mud, rock, clay, gravel, or sand. Individually, none of these compositions are of particular importance in attracting or holding bass. In many bodies of water there are areas where the bottom changes from one type to another that offer unique feeding opportunities. Bass can, for example, feed on minnows that sought to blend into a clay bottom, then move just a few feet onto a rock bottom to feed on crayfish.

The question is how, as surface-bound anglers, we might come to know the bottom's nature when it's covered by 20 feet of water. The nearest shoreline usually provides a clue. If there's a sandy beach-like area that abruptly becomes a rocky shoreline, it's a reasonable assumption that this circumstance continues for some distance away from shore. These transitional areas should be tested. As before, temperature and sunlight penetration provide strong reasons to suspect the depth that holds the bass. If we confine our casts to those depths and to areas of bottom-composition change we eliminate a lot of unproductive water. We can discard even more by realizing these conditions, when accompanied by some irregular feature, further attract ol' bucketmouth and his friends. Long stretches of flat bottom don't hold bass. A submerged hump, rock pile, submerged wood pile, creek channel, or stump patch provide cover and resulting security that can turn a transition area with comfortable water temperatures and sunlight penetration into a bona fide lunker factory.

In the 1960s we fished a central-Minnesota lake every summer that had a submerged island topped with emergent bulrushes. Like the other fishermen on the lake, we routinely tossed surface and shallow-running patterns at the edges and into the pockets of the rushes. The island was a productive stop early in the season, but it drew few bass after the end of June. These trips predated our locators so it took an old guide to show us that one side of the island was littered with old logs extending into the lake basin. Our guide friend used a bait-casting rod and baited specially designed weedless hooks with live frogs to fish the area. The technique was lethal. He caught an astonishing number of bass up to 20 inches from the logjam. At the time, our bass flies and equipment weren't very sophisticated. We cast large poppers and streamers, and had no sinking line, but our success there was good. It's a place we really need to revisit. We still talk of returning with full-sinking lines, short, heavy leaders with 16-pound tippets, and frog patterns to strip erratically above that log pile.

One deepwater presentation involves using a floating fly attached to full-sinking fly line. The fly must be a bit buoyant, but not to the point of failing to sink from the line's weight. A big Marabou Muddler works pretty well. Let the line settle to the bottom before imparting slow, irregular strips. The line snakes along the bottom, causing a bit of a disturbance, followed by the fly, which remains fully visible to the fish and free from hang-ups on the usual snags. Experiment with leader lengths to find just the right position in the water column for the fly, but short leaders of 4 to 6 feet are usually about right. Lifting the rod tip occasionally causes the fly to rise off the bottom before diving downward in pursuit of the sinking line.

The most obvious deepwater presentation utilizes a heavily weighted fly, a stout 6-foot leader, and sinking line. The idea is to maintain almost constant contact with the bottom. Usually, the more disturbances created along the bottom, the better. A covering of silt is common in most lakes and ponds. Sinking line and heavy, head-weighted flies snaked along the bottom cause little silt clouds as the flies are slowly dredged along. To bass, this signals something of significant heft has invaded their territory and warrants investigation. Even if the bottom is composed of clean gravel, the intermittent clicking sound created by the heavy fly's contact accomplishes the same end.

A good fly for working deep structure is the Batman, first conceived by Florida guide Capt. Russell Tharin and introduced to us by Florida-based tier Kevin Cohenour. It features wings on either side of the body, which move each time the fly is stripped or stopped. This is Captain Tharin's recipe:

Batman

Hook: Mustad 34011, size 4/0
Thread: Black flat nylon
Eyes: Gold dumbbell
Flash: Pearl Krystal Flash
Claws: Black Zonker strips, two 1-inch pieces
Body: Black Orvis Hi-density Crystal Chenille

Attach thread at bend. Secure dumbbell eyes at bend using "X' wraps. Cut 12 strands of Krystal Flash 3 inches long. Attach directly in front of eyes, long end pointing to the rear. Pull over eyes and secure using "X" wraps over eyes. Strip the fur from the front 1/4 inch of each Zonker strip to make a tag. Wind thread vertically around the far eye, then half hitch around the eye. Attach one Zonker strip to the front side of the eye. extending to the side, by the stripped tag, fur facing forward. Repeat for the near side eye. Ensure the wings are level on each side. With tying thread, make 2 half-hitches in front of the eyes. Attach a 12-inch length of chenille in front of eyes. Wind thread to hook eye. Add a drop of super glue to thread wraps over eyes. Make a vertical wrap with chenille around the eye on the far side. Cross thread over to near side and repeat. The claws should stand out on each side. Make an "X" wrap over top of eyes with chenille. Double wrap the shank with the chenille. Secure the chenille at the hook eye. Whip finish, cut thread and cement. Even the two Zonker-strip claws and trim Krystal Flash to 3/4 inch.

For this bottom fishing, we are partial to patterns made with lead barbell eyes. Barbell eyes are the creation of Tom Schmuecker, founder of Wapsi Fly, Inc. of Mountain Home, Arkansas. Tom was trying to perfect his Lead-eyed Bunny Booger and those remarkable barbells just kept evolving in his quest to further weight the fly. On our mid-depth flies we commonly use size "small" barbell eyes that are 1/36 ounce, but for bottom-bumping we switch to the medium size which weigh 1/24 ounce. They're manufactured in red, yellow, and pearl, all with black pupils. They also make a plain lead version to be painted by the tier. The Lead-eyed Bunny Booger is excellent for bottom fishing. Aside from getting down quickly and providing the desired dredging action on soft bottoms, when lead eyes are tied on top of the hook shank they cause the fly to ride hook-point up. It helps keep the fly out of trouble, but this characteristic must be taken into account in tying the fly. Here's the recipe:

Lead-Eyed Bunny Booger (chartreuse)

Hook: Straight eye, short shank

*Heavily weighted weedless Bunny Leeches offer just one of
many alternatives for deepwater fly fishing.*

Eyes: Lead, painted yellow with black pupils
Tail: Tapered rabbit fur strip, dyed chartreuse, skin side facing up
Body: Chartreuse cross-cut rabbit strip, wrapped around the hook shank
and in front of the eyes
Head: Red
Note: White, black, and olive Bunny Boogers are also effective.

Another barbell-eyed fly we use for deep fishing is our own Wilson's
Rattle Snake. It's 7 1/2 inches long and gets deep when tied with
medium barbell eyes, yet can be fished effectively within a foot of the
surface if tied using self-adhesive eyes. The fly should be fished with
quick jerks followed by pauses to activate the rattle and tail.

Wilson's Rattle Snake (purple)
Hook: Mustad 34007, 4/0
Thread: UNI Big Fly

Weed Guard: 25-pound stiff mono (tied double)
Rattles: Two glass rattle chambers (worm rattles)
Tail: Purple Edgewater Rat Tail Component
Body: Purple dyed rabbit strips
Eyes: Medium barbell eyes for deep fishing, or self-adhesive eyes for shallow fishing, red with black pupils
Head: Purple E-Z Shape Sparkle Body
Note: Chartreuse, raspberry and gray, and black all work well, too.

Sometimes it's necessary to imitate baitfish in deep water. Clousers have been the deepwater staple in most bass fly-fishers' boxes for years. Terry Tanner, Fly Fishing Specialist at Bass Pro Shops Outdoor World in Springfield, Missouri, uses his Clouser-style minnow imitation in gray when bass are feeding on shad, and switches to darker green shades when baitfish aren't active. Green shades also work well in moving water. Terry attaches the barbell eyes farther back on the hook shank than the original to achieve a more minnow-like action.

Tanner's Clouser Minnow
Hook: Mustad 455, size 1
Thread: Gray 6/0 pre-waxed
Eyes: Small brass barbell eyes with painted black pupils
Throat: Gray bucktail over craft fur over pearl Flashabou
Wing: Icelandic sheep hair over red hackle fibers

Kevin Cohenour of Pensacola, Florida created Clousers tied with white Orvis Super Hair wings so they could be colored on the spot with indelible markers to match the available baitfish. Hamilton Franz, who guides on Florida's phosphate pits at Bienville Plantation, adds stripes, flared gills, and color to them as the situation dictates. Hamilton also paints Kevin's Clear Clousers, tied 6 to 8 inches long, to match "worm of the year" colors.

We also use Wilson's Jointed Sally and Wilson's Bass Bully Tied with medium barbell eyes for bottom bouncing.

One of our favorite central Illinois lakes was a newer water supply lake of 250 acres. Its riprap-faced dam had clay that eventually yielded to the silt bottom at its base. The depth of the riprap was 12 feet and the clay extended another 4 feet before being overtaken by silt at the lake's floor. Bass used the riprap, especially the corners, to feed on crayfish on cloudy days or early and late when the sun's angle was lowest. On post-cold-front days with cloudless, sun-filled skies the bass dropped away from the riprap onto the clay apron. These deeper fish were usually in a pretty neutral feeding mood and could be difficult, but we knew if we were going to fish after a front moved through we'd encounter lots of bass just riding it out. Our best success here came when the boat was positioned near the dam and we cast into deeper water and let our sinking lines and heavy flies drop onto the silt. We crawled our flies slowly through the silt and hopped them up the clay embankment. When they clicked into the riprap without a strike, it was our signal to pick up and recast. If this tactic didn't connect, we tried a controlled drift that caused the fly to swing back and forth between the silt and riprap. It's our experience the latter technique is helpful in locating a concentration of fish along the line of the clay apron because we cover more ground using the controlled drift or trolling. Once a pod of fish is located, we find stationary casts disturb the fish less, and, consequently, cause more hookups.

Scientific studies, particularly one conducted by Southern Illinois University in the 1960s and early 1970s, have shown bass spend 90 percent of their time away from shoreline cover. Further, these extensive tagging studies have shown when largemouth bass moved to shoreline cover they returned, in spite of repeated capture, to the same area of shoreline. These studies, coupled with our own observations, convince us largemouth bass are strongly territorial, and deeper water is the home of most largemouth bass. It prompts us to speculate bass are equally territorial in their deeper haunts, but since electro-shocking is effective only in relatively shallow water, evidence is lacking.

Over the years we attempted to prove it, at least to our own satisfaction, by keeping extensive notes on bass we caught. One 15-inch fish was easily distinguishable from the others because it had a misshapen mandible. It was lying on a firm bottom under a shoreline willow when it fell in love with a yellow popper. We caught that fish four more times the same season, and three times the following year. Each of those encounters was over a submerged, weed-covered hump that rose to 9 feet with 12 feet of water on either side. The deepwater location wasn't more than 30 feet from our shoreline meeting place in a 37-acre pond. That bass answered a lot of questions for us. Clearly, it was a homebody and gobbling up the same fly didn't bother it at all. Of our seven encounters, it hit a size-4 yellow marabou streamer four times. Five hookups occurred on a yellow fly. Did it travel to the shoreline cover regularly? Did it move about the whole pond only to return to the submerged hump? Our speculation is it made forays to the same shallow area regularly, and we always expected to catch it there again. We also theorize the weed-covered hump provided for its needs pretty satisfactorily so it didn't stray far, but we'll never know for sure. Because we can't observe deeper water as readily as shallow water, even with sophisticated electronic devices, these answers and others remain elusive. We never encountered the fish again.

Trolling and controlled drifting often provide the best initial approach to deep water because they allow us to cover lots of bass territory efficiently. One key to successful deep trolling is allowing the fly and line to sink completely to the bottom before moving the boat. In a controlled drift situation it can be difficult to overcome the breeze and get your fly down quickly enough. Using the trolling motor to slowly move the boat against the wind solves these problems. When the fly and line touch down, simply turn off the motor and begin the drift. Also pay careful attention to the location where fish contact was made, but this isn't always as easy as it sounds. The line is draped at an angle toward bottom some distance from the boat. It becomes increasingly confusing in direct relation to the distance from shore, so the more familiar the angler is with the area, the better. Still, a means of returning to the spot is necessary. This is a problem best solved by two anglers fishing from the same boat. The fisherman other than the one playing the fish should immediately be alerted to locational landmarks on shore.

For many years we've used a method of returning to the same location on the water. Choose two prominent, aligned land features on one shore and two aligned land features on another shore a right angle to the first. Note the point where the two lines intersect your position so you can return there easily. The method isn't without pitfalls. Wind can cause problems in exact alignment. Subsequent removal of one of your "permanent" landmarks can unravel the whole system. Misplacing your notebook can cost you dozens of productive offshore areas.

Global Positioning Systems are quite new to the fishing world, but they're an accurate means of determining locations of structure and catches on large waters. Anglers can input markers for landmarks and events to assist them in returning to the same spots, but it's still necessary to log the data on a notepad, particularly if fishing several different lakes or rivers is involved. They're the ultimate fishing log accessories, and G.P.S. system units can be rather expensive.

Determining your position by whatever method allows you to troll or drift the area again. If another hookup is made, it might be best to anchor within casting distance and fan cast the area. Before leaving the spot, run over it several times with your locator to determine what it is that attracts the bass.

Most of our deep trolling and drifting is done with a fly that's our own adaptation of Lefty Kreh's famous Deceiver pattern. Our fly utilizes a different body and head but the same tail and wings as the original.

E-Z Deceiver (red)
Hook: Mustad 34007, size 1/0 to 4/0
Thread: UNI Big Fly
Tail: 2 red and 2 orange grizzly saddle hackles tied in at the hook bend to extend 1 1/2 times the length of the hook shank
Underbody: Red Krystal Flash wrapped around the hook shank (silver also works well)
Body: Silver Flak Jelly Rope
Back and belly: Red over orange bucktail extending half the length of the hook shank
Head: E-Z Shape Sparkle Body, red

Eyes: Small yellow decal eyes applied when head is nearly dry

Note: The E-Z Deceiver can be tied with a weed guard, casts well, and can be fished as a streamer. It's also effective in red/yellow, orange/olive, chartreuse, white, and purple. The saltwater hook provides some weighting, but we always fish it on full-sinking line.

Flies for deep water available over the counter are Clousers, the Marabou Muddler, the Bunny Leech (we like purple and chartreuse), and heavily weighted crayfish flies.

Locators And Fishfinders

Locators can be invaluable in locating fish-holding structure, and that's just as important to fly-casters as tournament pros. We bought our first locator in 1970. It was one of Lowrance's "little green boxes," a flasher unit that required lots of practice to learn to interpret the strange flashing lights. In the beginning, we used it on a 35-acre pond we already knew quite well. Its first importance was confirming what we already knew about the bottom of our pond. Then the locator began surprising us by revealing some humps and depressions we hadn't previously known were there. Very soon, we regarded our new locator as magic. We even learned to see fish and could distinguish larger fish from smaller ones. Like all locator neophytes, we expected to find bass structure, see the bass, isolate the larger ones, and without major difficulty, catch them.

Needless to say, it doesn't quite work that way. Even with today's high-resolution electronics, it's a poor tactic to try to focus on individual fish. That can quickly raise the frustration meter into the red zone. Instead, learn to get the most from your locator by getting to know the capabilities of your model. Today's flasher units are far superior to the antique we first used, and graph units can provide an instant understanding with little interpretation. The most important information a locator provides is showing the underwater structures that attract and hold bass. Fish the structure, not the fish. When fish are seen on the screen, pay particular attention to their position. That's the real value to seeing fish. If the fish are up in, or on, the structure, they're in a positive feeding mood. If they're low and in or under a weed bed or tight to the trunks in standing timber they're probably negative, and very difficult to entice. Still, you'll know whether to "tickle the edges" of structure or try to present something weedless right down in the dense structure.

The bottom line is that locators teach you more about your water than you knew, and likely more about largemouth bass. This is especially true regarding fish movement—where fish go in summer's heat or when a cold front moves through.

In addition to a locator, use your own powers of observation. Look at the nearest shoreline to determine, as best you can, the bottom content. Then look for areas with the same structure at the same depths. From that reconnaissance, discovering several hotspots is a possibility well worth the effort. If the area proves to be a good producer, it's a good idea to keep a notepad in the boat to write down all the pertinent information so you can return to the area easily. Record the position and landmarks, as well as weather conditions, time of year, and water temperatures. When facing similar conditions, return to the site of earlier successes. Don't forget to check the area under other conditions. You might have located a major hotspot.

Targeting Deep Structure

Bass in deepwater structure might often see a lot of large, heavy hardware moving near their lairs. If we can present flies to them in an enticing manner, they can be fooled into making good memories for us.

The bases of bluffs are prime deep locations for bass. Position the boat tight to the bluff and fish parallel to it with 50- to 60-foot casts. Let the line bow laterally to 20 feet deep, then strip and allow the fly to resettle.

Fish the ends of points from shallow to deep by utilizing long casts and short strips. Allow the fly to settle to the desired depth and retrieve it upward. If there's no wind, it's possible to fish deep to shallow, but longer strips are necessary to keep the fly from hang-ups. Anchoring the boat in 20 feet of water is a problem, so a trolling motor must be used or use a controlled drift.

There are two methods of fishing submerged creek channels: stationary casting and controlled drifting. Make stationary casts to the area you're fishing. Mark the area with floats because it's easy to lose the location of the channel. Choose sleek flies with few appendages, such as Woolly Buggers, Deceivers, and worm and leech patterns. Keep the line as straight as possible and remove all slack immediately. If you're employing a controlled drift, let the fly get all the way down before starting the motor. Use short bursts and allow the fly to resettle. Troll into the wind to slow the fly's movement for increased depth.

Troll flies in zigzag paths along the bottom and the deep edges of riprap. In a stationary situation, cast to depths of 20 feet and hop the fly progressively shallower. If there is deep water at the corners where riprap meets the shoreline or directly in front of the spillway where there might have be an old creek channel, stationary casts present flies best. Clousers in crayfish and minnow colors, dark Woolly Buggers, and dark leeches can be most productive.

The ends of docks are good situations for bowing. Position tight to the dock's end and cast in line with the structure, which could be old Christmas trees, natural breaklines, or dock pilings. Estimate the length of the cast needed to bow the line into the structure, raise the rod tip, and let the fly flutter down.

Submerged humps can be fished with stationary casts if surface floats are used to mark the humps' locations. Minnow, leech, and worm imitations are good choices. Troll or employ a controlled drift to fish them, too.

The ends of deadfalls can be good locations if the trees extend from shore and their branches spread. Casts with weedless flies to open areas between branches can be the most successful because other anglers are likely to avoid them. The outside edges offer bass many ambush points, and they should be fished relatively shallow to deep or vice versa. If the deadfall is fresh with lots of branches and leaves intact, position to cast just beyond the treetop at a right angle to its trunk and allow the line to bow in deep water past the outermost branches. Another alternative is vertical jigging.

Secondary breaklines are those beyond the first or primary shallow breaklines. In northern lakes, secondary breaklines are often located where the last vegetation is found before encountering deep water. This can be deep water, depending on sunlight penetration. Use bowing or a controlled drift with worm and leech imitations, and big Woolly Buggers.

In many bodies of water, deep largemouth haunts remain unexplored regions. This is especially true for fly-fishers. Success requires full-sinking line, carefully selected flies, and a little patience. A good locator can be very helpful, but it cannot replace the eye of an observant fly-fisher. After gathering as much information as possible, it's a good idea to visualize the underwater situation, then fish carefully while keeping the line and fly under control. Be alert for any suggestion of a strike, and set the hook in deep water with real gusto. If you can unlock the secrets of the deep water on your lake or pond, you will very likely catch fish through the entire season.

Chapter 8

Time, Weather, and Locational Patterns

If it's true that time spent fishing isn't deducted from our life spans, we'll surely live to be two hundred. We believe the best time to go fishing is anytime you can.

Many seasons ago, a close friend drove over 6 hours to fish with us for a couple of days. The weather had been stable for two weeks and the early-summer bass fishing had bordered on sensational. The day before our friend's arrival brought a storm, and the day of our initial outing was cool, clear, and bright—classic post-cold front conditions. The results were predictable. We fished two ponds with little success before loading a car-top boat to head for a village water supply lake. We fished the little lake's best cover and spent more time searching with the locator. Disconsolate and drifting aimlessly while contemplating other options, our visitor cast to the base of a concrete tower that served as the lake's pumping station. There was a 20-foot hole at the base of the tower and a steep mud slope to the nearest shoreline. There was little to attract or hold bass. Our guest's fly settled along the mud embankment at about 8 feet without incident, but just as he began to return his lure the line felt heavy and he set the hook. The location and bulldogging fight convinced us it was a catfish until its massive silver sides told a different tale. The fight occurred over deep, open water free of snags and obstructions. His heavy rod bowed deeply well into the butt. Toward the end, the tired behemoth wallowed on the surface before allowing itself to be drawn toward the boat. When we were finally able to grasp its lower jaw, it was measured at 19 1/2 inches, then released. Two more hours of casting produced no strikes. It was our friend's only fish of the trip and he speaks of it still. What a shame it would have been had we calculated the odds of catching fish at near zero and decided against making the trip.

There are times, however, that can be recommended as potentially excellent. One of these times is in early spring before the spawn.

Largemouth Bass Calendar

Pre-spawn	55-62 degrees	Bass move shallow and prepare to spawn
Spawn	62-65 degrees	Males escort ripened females to nest
Post-spawn	65-68 degrees	Recovery period. Females not feeding males guarding nest
Summer	68-80+degrees	Daily movement patterns
Fall	70-55 degrees	Bass feed in shallows. Building winter reserves
Cold Water	55-32 degrees	Bass deep, activity reduced

Time

As cold-blooded creatures, the activities of largemouth bass are governed by water temperature that regulates its seasonal calendar. While the temperature ranges aren't absolute and not all bass respond alike, the largemouth calendar provides a general understanding of seasonal movement. Years ago, we had a hand-held, battery-operated temperature gauge with a probe that lowered into the water. At the touch of a button we knew the temperature at any depth we selected. It's important to know the temperature where the fish are located. Surface temperature, therefore, is meaningless.

When the shallows warm in spring, bass yield to their instincts to propagate the species. Male largemouths respond first. As water temperatures rise into the high forties, they slowly move to a staging area. Staging areas are breaklines, or areas where structure or bottom composition changes abruptly, i.e. a sharp drop-off. At about 50 degrees, their activity along this breakline just off their spawning flats increases. They're hungry, competitive, and even combative. Male bass located in staging areas are certainly catchable. The higher the temperature, the more active they are. As the water nears the mid-fifties, they become quite aggressive. Bass in staging areas are particularly sensitive to weather changes. An arctic blast can send them back to deep water. A warming trend, on the other hand, can cause them to move cautiously toward their spawning grounds. The distance between the staging area and the shallows is usually not far. Spawning areas can be in water so shallow that dorsal fins can be seen above the surface. At the other extreme, in clear lakes the spawn can take place as deep as 8 feet or more.

Bass are not so predictable that they always respond to the same stimuli in the same way, so activities associated with specific temperatures shouldn't be written in stone. Although most sexually mature male bass are motivated to move toward spawning grounds as water temperatures reach 55 degrees, some jump the gun and others lag behind. Still, our efforts are best served if we focus on the majority. Roughly then, from 55 to 62 degrees male bass prepare their spawning beds among many nearly interconnected within a spawning colony. They use their tails to fan silt from the beds and excavate a round depression that's eventually about 3 feet in diameter. Bass beds lack the neatness and uniformity of bluegill beds. Males also pick up debris with their mouths and deposit it outside the nest. At this time they aren't necessarily motivated to feed, and yet it's this pre-spawn period that causes bass to be most vulnerable to anglers.

Actually, two fishing possibilities exist during pre-spawn. First, anglers can appeal to aggressive male bass by bringing some annoying

The largemouth bass's thrashing, leaping fight allows
much of the action to remain visible.

nest invader to the attention of nest builders. Male bass grab nearly any-thing now, but set the hook quickly because they expel foreign objects promptly and get back to their duties. The aggressive and combative nature of bass on the nests often enables anglers to catch and release many. Surface flies and floater/divers can be very productive if the spawning beds are shallow enough. Vertical drop and mid-depth flies can also be effective. Even bottom bouncers have a place in this presentation.

The second fishing opportunity involves larger females located along the first major breakline. Look for offshore cover near spawning beds. Females are naturally larger than males of their year-class, and are heavy with eggs. This is a good opportunity to catch the season's largest fish, but be forewarned; these old gals aren't much interested in feeding and certainly won't chase anything. Vertical drop flies, precisely located and imparted with slow movement, can be the keys. Considerable discipline is required to stick with a plan to catch a big pre-spawn female while other fishermen corner the action.

Repeated sudden cold snaps can provoke a retreat from the spawning beds and repeatedly foiled attempts can cause the whole process to be abandoned for the year.

Again, using approximate temperatures, the spawn itself takes place between 62 and 65 degrees. When males escort ripened females to their nests to fertilize the eggs, neither is interested in feeding. After the females deposit their eggs, they slowly retreat into deeper water and spend the next several days recovering from their rigorous activity. They're nearly impossible to catch during this post-spawn period, but males are another story. They instinctively provide the only protection and parenting eggs and young fry receive. As the water continues to warm, the eggs hatch in 7 to ten days under normal conditions, while papa bass hangs around to defend the nest against intrusion. Any fly or lure entering its territory will likely be smashed. Again, vertical drop and mid-depth flies work best.

Eventually, the parenting instinct wears thin and male bass charge through their tightly clustered offspring gulping as many as possible. This act causes surviving fry to disperse quickly and seek protection among vegetation and wood structure. It's a precarious time for tiny bass and few survive to maturity.

One of bass fishing's most difficult times occurs immediately after the post-spawn and usually continues for a week to ten days. They move to their summer homes and rest from the rigors of the spawn. While most of the fish are experiencing this transitional downtime, there are always some stragglers left near the spawning sites and some early birds that are into their summer routine. It's still possible to catch fish in those locations, but it's usually a slow process that seems hard to fathom when weather and water temperatures are so perfect.

Much has been written about the summer migration habits of largemouth bass. While it's true many fish stay in or near deep structure, most of the time and move shallow to feed during periods of low light; some bass remain shallow nearly all the time if suitable shade, cover, and water temperatures are available. The percentage of bass that are in one or the other of these summer haunts is dependent upon how much of each is attainable and varies greatly in different bodies of water.

In summer, there are several periods that merit special consideration. All of them involve times when light penetration into the water is substantially reduced.

Night fishing can provide relief from oppressive heat and may yield the season's biggest bass.

Early and late in the day, when the sun provides enough light that bass can see their prey, can usually be fished more successfully than midday. Depending on water clarity, wind, and the availability of suitable overhead cover, bass can seek the protection of deep water. They are most active shortly before, during, and shortly after sunrise in periods of extreme heat because water temperatures reach their coolest at daybreak. If bass are reluctant to feed due to excessive temperatures, the best chance for success is when the surface is coolest and light penetration is low. Topwater flies and floater/divers can be especially good.

Sunset is another low light opportunity. It doesn't provide heat relief for bass, but they can avoid the sunlight and hunt for sustenance.

Another low-light condition highly prized by bassers is the overcast day. Even days when humidity makes the sky appear hazy allow bass to locate in shallower positions. The sun's rays are reduced by moisture in the atmosphere so largemouths are more comfortable near the surface. Cold fronts, conversely, remove the humidity and bass retreat from unrestrained light. On dark, gloomy days the best opportunity to catch shallow bass is during the brightest period, usually midday when sunlight penetration is low but their visibility is high. Bass that stuck their heads into the darkness of heavy weeds reposition themselves so they can wait in ambush. They're able to see more clearly for greater distances; consequently, they might be more likely to dart out from their lairs to grab likely looking morsels.

The longer a period of reduced sunlight penetration lasts, the more aggressive bass can become. But when the intense direct sunlight returns after a long overcast period, the bass population is well fed. For a while, it's not vital they make themselves uncomfortable by exposure to sun or heat. Summer is a time of abundance; food is readily available, and the menu is diverse. Bass become very lazy. Larger fish ambush a convenient, sizeable meal or two then remain nearly motionless while digesting their food and observing their environment. Conditions need to be agreeable again before they're prompted to increase their alertness for prey. In the meantime, they feed only when the opportunity presents itself. An injured minnow fluttering within inches of a bass's gaping mouth is still vulnerable as long as inhaling is the only energy expenditure required.

Nighttime

An extended period of darkness occurs once each day, of course, and bass utilize it. Immediately after post-spawn, bass quickly orient their lifestyle to the ease of summer's abundance. For a large proportion of adult bass, this means hunting under cover of darkness using their excellent senses to detect sound and vibration.

The spin-casting and bait-casting segments of the fishing world have long understood this and learned to function efficiently at night, but for most bass fly-fishers nighttime is alien territory. In July and August, fishing much of the nation's bass water is far more comfortable at midnight than at noon. After dark, winds usually calm to gentle breezes that are far more manageable for the fly-caster. If the sky is clear, moonlight is sometimes adequate for fishing and navigation.

Fishing at night with fly rods can be more productive than daytime fishing, but it's easy to understand the necessity of having an intimate knowledge of the area before attempting a trip there in darkness. Structure that's easily recognizable in daylight appears much different at night.

If the fishing location is a small pond, move slowly and carefully, and know in advance where your tippet changes and flies are kept. Short, accurate casts are best. Use artificial light sparingly and keep it off the water.

If the water is large enough to launch a boat, try using black lights. That's how bait-casters function so well under cover of darkness, but they have one advantage. Their fluorescent lines look like rope in black light. Fly-fishers don't yet have fluorescent lines, but some light-colored fly lines can be seen with black light fairly well. Surprisingly, white-colored lines might not be easier to see. We recommend testing your fly lines for visibility before planning a nighttime fishing trip. A monofilament named Amnesia is quite visible for several yards under black light, and it can be added between the fly line and leader for strike detection.

Black lights mount on the side of the boat and illuminate a limited area of the water's surface and attending structure. They emit enough light to change flies, tippets, and reel spools. They also illuminate fly line well enough to detect twitches from the subtle takes of submerged flies.

Surface or mid-depth flies with rattles are good choices for night fishing because bass depend upon their sense of hearing and their ability to detect vibrations at night. It's easiest, however, to use surface flies and floater/divers that we can see. As exciting as a surface strike is in full daylight, it's even more thrilling at night. Surface presentations at night are best using relatively short casts to familiar cover and weedless flies to minimize unwanted hookups. Darkened conditions would seem to call for dark-colored flies. That poses no problem if you've selected wet flies, but it can be troublesome when poppers are the fare. They become invisible to the caster, which hinders their manipulation. We often use white, yellow or chartreuse poppers so we can see them better, and they seem nearly as effective as dark ones. Adding stripes of fluorescent paint to the topsides of our poppers and floater/divers also works well.

Nocturnal habits of sizeable largemouth bass just can't be ignored, and they shouldn't be conceded to other fishermen. Black lights work for fly-fishers and enable them to not only catch more bass but bigger ones as well. Here are the problems we've encountered and our observations. First, some black lights' connecting wires can be too short to reach farther than the middle of the boat and wiring supplements to extend them are an additional expense. Second, when buying black lights get the brightest available and consider using one for each end of the boat. Third, we've been disappointed with the distance at which fly lines remain visible. Fourth, light, black or otherwise, attracts insects by the thousands. Keep the repellant and hand-cleaner handy.

Much more exploration into nighttime warmwater fly-fishing still needs to be done.

Autumn

The progressively shorter days and cooler evenings of autumn put large-mouths on the move. They spend an increasing amount of time feeding, moving to the shallows for longer periods, and even foraging for food. In reservoirs, some follow large schools of shad (see Chapter 2). When bass revisit the shallows, it's the last opportunity to cast poppers, sliders, wakers, and floater/divers. Minnow-imitating colors with white and silver work well, but pay attention to fly size. As water temperatures cool, drop down to smaller sizes. Those 3/0 and 4/0 monsters we recommended for spring and summer can be put in the bottom of your tackle bag for the rest of the year. Sizes 2 to 6 do much better in autumn and winter.

As the surface temperatures steadily cool, bass move to the next deeper available cover until the lake turns over before heading to their winter quarters. Points that slope gradually to deep water are autumn's best targets. Bass aren't always located in deep water during the autumn period. Keep in mind that fish are dependent upon water temperature rather than air temperature.

Winter

In small ponds, bass can locate in the basin near the dam in the deepest available water during the coldwater period. In natural lakes, they can be on deep, submerged humps or at the base of the deepest breakline. Impoundment bass can take up residence at the bases of bluffs, in deeper creek channels, or suspend in the tops of standing timber. In rivers, they almost certainly reside in the deepest holes, and near a spring if one exists.

Vegetation, particularly in shallow water, no longer offers them warmth and food. Dying plants deplete oxygen from the water, and sunlight penetration is often too intense in the now thin cover.

Winter largemouth bass fly-fishing takes on a whole new personality that redefines slow. In ponds, cast full-sinking lines and size-6 darkly colored flies into the deepest holes. The retrieve needs to crawl the fly along the bottom at a snail's pace. The same tactic applies to rivers. In impoundments, the same dark-colored, small flies are lowered to the bases of bluffs, into creek channels, and the extended branches of standing timber, then yo-yoed slowly by keeping the line and weighted fly under direct control. No freefalling here. That moves the fly too quickly to interest the bass.

An exception to typical winter largemouth fishing is warmwater discharge lakes. Power plants use the lake's water and return it at a constant temperature. We know of one such reservoir where the temperatures rarely dip below 63 degrees. This dramatically alters winter fishing, but it causes some new problems. Cold air temperatures can create a cold, gray, moist fog that can even form frost on boat carpet. Even when it doesn't, it's a penetrating type of cold that requires heavily insulated clothing.

Small flies fished slowly over deeper structure prevail here as short days cause the bass population to respond to winter conditions. Certainly, the bass are more active, and conventional casting replaces yo-yoing as the recommended tactic. One additional benefit is the pre-spawn occurs in these waters as soon as days begin to lengthen, and there can be several additional "false spawning runs" to the shallows by male bass.

Weather

Weather conditions have an enormous impact on our fishing. They dictate where the bass are located at any given time, and they affect our presentation methods, casts, comfort, and even our safety.

A couple of Novembers ago we launched our boat on a local reservoir. Our mission was catching muskie, and we had tied some extra-large streamers for the trip. The sky was heavily overcast and a stiff breeze made the main lake choppy. We planned to fish the stump-littered mouth of a large protected cove. A friend had caught a small muskie there the previous week, and we were optimistic as we tossed big hair-wing streamers. We had immediate success and landed several large fish, but none were muskies. They were all largemouth bass that slammed our flies and fought well. We entered the cove and continued along its winding course, and as the air seemed cooler we zipped our heavy coats. Wind swayed the treetops on the ridge, but the fishing action had our full attention. As we motored back toward the cove's mouth we saw the main lake covered in white caps. The temperature had dropped 15 degrees. Suddenly, our late-season lark was clearly dangerous, and making it to the boat ramp was only the beginning of the problems we faced. We loaded the boat as breakers crashed over the stern. Our insulated clothing was soaked and freezing, and ice had formed on the concrete ramp. We were lucky to take out without mishap, but it was a solid reminder of the importance of constantly monitoring weather changes.

Just as wind became our nemesis that day, in smaller doses it can be our ally. Steady breezes aimed at good bass structures wash in a constant food supply. Always the opportunists, bass line up facing the waves and select their meals from a variety of helpless creatures. Wind and wave action can pin a school of minnows against the shore. Streamers cast across the wind and retrieved broadside to the waiting bass are attacked aggressively.

If the wind becomes so strong fishing is no longer comfortable, wave action is probably too turbulent for shallow fish as well. When this occurs, look for a high bank that shields the water from the wind. Fish related to nearby wind-beaten structure can move into a leeward area to ride it out. Fish obvious, well-structured areas carefully. If sheltered water doesn't harbor good structure, try trolling with minnow imitations to see if the bass have moved into the protected area. If you're able to score, stop and fan-cast the area more carefully.

Another breezy-day tactic involves using the wind to blow your craft along a prospective piece of cover. Adjust your position with thrusts from the trolling motor. A controlled drift allows for trolling or making casts along the structure. Mid-depth flies are frequently best for this situation because it's easier to control the fly's depth. It's possible in relatively shallow cover to troll or drift using floating line, but when fishing depth exceeds 4 feet, sinking line offers the best presentation.

Allow wind to aid your cause, but don't permit it to affect your safety. Despite the weather forecast, keep a wary eye on changes that could turn a good time into disaster. Don't be misled into believing that an inadequate craft can handle big waters. It can serve passably in calm water, but become life threatening in the wind. It's also prudent to have enough horsepower to return to your launch area quickly.

One of the most demanding fishing situations occurs after a strong front has moved through the area. There can be storms either ahead of the front, behind it, or both. Clearing weather gives the appearance of a return to normal. Bright blue skies, lots of sunshine, and cool temperatures are the order of the day. Sounds like a great day to head for the lake, but it's usually a signal that the bass will be difficult.

If post cold-front conditions occur during the spawning process, bass will likely back off the beds. The culprit this time isn't bright sunlight. The problem is the sudden temperature drop that can cause the water's warmth to dissipate in the shallows. If a temperature drop materializes, bass retreat into deeper water and wait for a warming trend before resuming their activities.

In the summertime it's excessive light penetration that ruins the day. Bass remain along the same pieces of structure, but put their heads into the thickest weeds or beneath submerged tree limbs with indifference. Anglers who insist on bucking the odds need to fish very tight to the structure and move their flies deliberately. Vertical jigging or yo-yoing in, or immediately adjacent to, thick cover can provide the only opportunities for hookups.

When confronted with classic cold front conditions, the best option can be night fishing. Over the years we've traveled long distances to fish hallowed bass water only to discover a front was moving through, and the time we'd reserved was lousy. A little advanced planning, light-colored lines, and a black light could have saved those trips.

Possibly the most difficult weather condition with which anglers must cope is what we call "sundance." It's the period when small, fast-moving clouds shield the sun from direct contact with the water for several minutes, and then the sun suddenly shines brightly for a few more minutes before other clouds obscure it again. This situation poses a problem because a bass has an immoveable iris in its eye, so the fish must physically move to compensate. Sundance is so changeable bass can't begin to feed at a depth where they feel safe. Even if they're hungry, after several frustrated attempts they go into hiding until the weather condition passes. The only solution is fishing deep enough that the bass's vision isn't a factor. In stained water, that can be only 5 or 6 feet, but in clear water, 20 feet might not be enough. Persistent fishermen should treat sundance like any other bright, sunlit situation. Cast very precisely and work flies slowly in dense cover.

Snow, sleet, and rain are merely inconvenient. All can be dealt with if we're dressed properly, and if the amounts of precipitation are moderate. During inclement weather, it's possible, even probable, that no adjustment in fishing location or presentation is necessary. The question that must be answered is: what's the change in the fish's environment? Snow, sleet, and rain favorably alter the amount of light penetration, but water temperature changes might not be radical. Surface flies can be rendered ineffective by rain as the disturbance to the upper layer of water increases. Otherwise, keep casting—the fish are already wet and, perhaps, cold.

The optimum weather condition for fishing is a falling barometer. This means a cold front is on the way. Bass might not even be aware of the change in water pressure, but the lake's microorganisms are affected and float to the surface. Minnows move immediately near the surface or into the shallows to feed and largemouth bass naturally follow. Moving water is less affected because current influences the water pressure. However, the slack areas of rivers preferred by largemouths will experience a less dramatic, but similar, effect.

Another weather condition favorable to bass fishermen is a period of stable weather. Stable weather is the same set of conditions day after day. This allows the fish to establish a predictable routine.

The first indication that weather conditions are about to change is usually a shift in the wind. It blows from a different direction, the velocity increases, or it becomes variable. We can no longer describe the weather as stable, and fish change their habits accordingly. They might simply move to utilize the new wind, or if a major storm follows, the majority can retreat to a deeper piece of structure to hide or suspend until the weather stabilizes once more. Summer-season bassing depends upon finding fish quickly, fishing the same places with the same types of flies and presentations as long as stable weather lasts, and then waiting for the weather to stabilize again after an interruption.

Establishing a Pattern

On any fishing trip, the first order of business is locating a population of catchable bass. To do so requires analyzing a set of prevailing fishing conditions called a "pattern." Sunlight penetration, water clarity, location of prey species, wind speed and direction, and water temperature top the list. Observation of current and immediately past weather conditions provides some clues. Taking the water temperature at various depths helps, too. For larger waters, consult a map looking for cover within the preferred comfort zone for bass at that season, then turn on the locator and find those areas before presenting flies that fit the situation. This can mean representing a particular prey species that's expected to be found there. Crayfish imitations can be used to fish an 8- to 12-foot deep riprap dam. It might be necessary to choose flies with weed guards if you've identified the deep end of a brushy deadfall as the bass's preferred haunt.

Only fish contact tells you the set of conditions under which bass can be caught. Understanding the pattern and focusing efforts on similar situations in other parts of the lake, pond, or river increases the likelihood of duplicating the catch. Success with the pattern likely continues until some detail of the set of conditions changes.

The pattern can be large yellow poppers in the backs of shallow black-bottomed coves on a lake's west side where the water has reached 60 degrees due to long sun and wave exposure. It could be heavy, dark-colored flies slowly stripped in 12 feet of water into stump patches along main lake points under overcast skies. The pattern can involve banging solid-headed flies into rocks along a riprap dam. The importance of finding the key triggering factor cannot be understated. On most days it will determine the angler's success or lack of it.

Many times, fishermen can identify the structure they believe holds bass, but isolating the correct depth, presentation method, retrieve, and type, size and color of fly is problematic. All we can do is fish through the problem-solving process using logic to eliminate less likely options. It's helpful to utilize the buddy system. One angler can use a different type and color of fly and fish another part of the same structure. For example, one casts shallow-running flies to the inside edge of a weedline while the other strips a heavy fly on sinking line along the face of the weeds. As soon as a pattern can be established, the information can be shared, and both can fish the same flies in the same manner along the same type of structure. The buddy system maximizes the efficiency of the fishing process and allows both anglers opportunities to increase the number of hookups.

Professional bass tournament competitors always spend as much time as possible "pre-fishing" the lake where the competition takes place in an attempt to locate as many established patterns as possible. During the tournament, they can focus on catching fish they already know are there. Even if they're thrown a curve by drastic weather changes, they can look at maps and locator screens to decide the most logical movements of their bass. The same rules apply to fly-fishers. Put the pieces of the puzzle together and detect patterns for catchable largemouth bass on small waters, moving waters, and large lakes. Any angler might happen to be in the right place at the right time and catch the biggest or the most bass, but, day in and day out, the angler who's able to discover the pattern catches more large bass.

Goodey's Secret

Over forty-five years ago, Bert's Barber Shop was a rich place to spend Saturday afternoons. Wicker chairs creaked, the pungent fragrance of hair tonic mingled with heavy blue cigar smoke, and Harry Caray rhapsodized, regularly punctuated by static buzzing, about the St. Louis Cardinals from a wooden Philco radio. The conversation always centered on fishing. A young boy might have confused it with heaven.

One early spring afternoon a muffled query came from beneath a steaming cloth.

"Seen the new fishin' lures over at Wright's Hardware Store?"

Bert grunted that he hadn't and added, "'Course a man can't ketch no bass on a cold day like this no matter what he uses."

Bushy eyebrows belonging to a man known only as "Goodey" raised from behind the latest copy of *Field & Stream*. "Sure can, I caught a nice mess just a coupla hours ago."

Inevitably a heated argument ensued and a not-so-friendly wager was placed. Goodey rushed outside, and the bell above the door of the shop clanged with annoyance. He could be seen opening the trunk of his Studebaker through the expansive shop window, and he quickly returned carrying a washtub containing genuine lunkers.

The audience acquired a respectful tone, and most regarded the catch as a miracle of biblical proportions. Several tried to dislodge his secret, but before collecting his wager Goodey only mumbled something about the water being warmer than the air.

Not all of what had been learned was yet understood, but the education of a lifelong bass fisherman had begun. Experience acquired from trial and error sustains the process, which continues.

Chapter 9

Beyond the Catch

Okay, the bass have been located, the right rod, line, leader, fly, and presentation used, and several fish have been caught. Is there more? Actually, yes.

Releasing Bass

How short-sighted it is to catch prized game fish like largemouth bass and fail to release them to propagate the species, control prey through their feeding activity, and live to grow and fight another day. It's self-limiting, of course, but it's also downright selfish. Nearly every informed fisherman understands the need for it, though many fail to take the painfully slow growth rates of largemouth bass into account. Even under optimum reservoir conditions, 3 years are required to grow a largemouth of 12 to 15 inches.

When fishing pressure creams the large bass of any water the natural balance of a healthy ecosystem is destroyed. Small and mid-sized sunfish aren't harvested. They quickly overpopulate, and the carrying capacity of the water is redistributed. Instead of good numbers of large bass that are able to control the sunfish population, the same number of pounds of stunted sunfish and bass fill the void. It's a poor trade, and the same anglers who depleted the lunker factory in the first place move on to over-harvest other waters. The whole chain of events can take a surprisingly short time. Small waters are particularly vulnerable, but even enormous lakes are victimized by the same meat hog mentality.

Lake Fork, Texas, is widely regarded as the best big bass fishery in the United States today. More than 350 largemouths of at least 10 pounds come from its waters each spring. It's an optimum environment with phenomenal growth rates, but one reason it continues to be regarded as blue-ribbon water is that guides, marinas, and resorts have encouraged catch-and-release around those celebrated waters.

The truth is not every release is a good one. Far from it. The good news is both the basic method and the terminal tackle used in fly-fishing are more conducive to releasing healthy fish. Live bait and treble hooks cause unnecessarily invasive hookups.

Everywhere we fish, we witness bass literally thrown onto the water's surface after hooks have been torn from their mouths. This practice, based on the assumption that bass are so mean and tough they can survive anything, are as far off course as the idea that there's an unlimited supply everywhere just beneath the water's surface. Largemouth bass can be less delicate than other freshwater species, but all fish can experience stress, shock, and death. A sensible approach to largemouth bass preservation is needed.

First, play the bass in a reasonably expedient way. It doesn't have to be rushed unnecessarily. When the fish is ready to be landed, lead it to hand. With wet hands to prevent harm to the fish's protective slime, grab its lower jaw with the thumb on the upper part of the lip and the forefinger thrust along the lower portion. This lipping technique immobilizes a bass and quiets its thrashing, but don't risk damaging its mouth by bending the lower jaw so its tongue protrudes. Try to keep the fish in a vertical position. If it's possible, leave the fish immersed in the water and back the hook out so it can easily swim away. If a landing net must be used, make it a fine mesh, knotless catch-and-release net. Minimal handling greatly enhances the bass's chances of survival. Want pictures? No problem, but be quick about it. Keep the fish submerged

There's simply no reason to kill a great game fish.

and breathing naturally, then lift it from the water with as little additional handling as possible. A photo or two are possible as long as the bass is put back into the water before each snap of the shutter. In moving waters, be sure to release the fish where there's a break in the current or in the stillest water possible. Make sure it's revived before the release by gently moving it back and forth to allow water to pass over its gills. Be proud to make your release a tribute to this legendary fighter's survival.

Another practice that unnecessarily costs the lives of many big bass is weighing the trophy. Weighing causes far too much fish-handling and involves the invasive practice of attaching the bass to the weighing device. The bass spends a long time out of the water and builds lactic acid in its muscle tissue that can be lethal. Measuring is a far surer and less damaging method of determining fish size. If we're told about a 5-pound catch, it's difficult to visualize, but when someone reports a 20-inch trophy we can completely appreciate the catch. Float tube and boat fishermen should make certain a tape measure is permanently mounted to allow a quick and accurate confirmation and expedient release. Bank stalkers and wading anglers should carry a tape measure in their vests or pockets. Universal acceptance of measuring trophies as opposed to weighing will save many large fish for all to enjoy catching again and again.

As for the practice of not releasing the bigger fish, well . . . it's inexcusable. There's just not a good reason to keep big largemouth bass. If occasionally the angler wants to keep some for the frying pan, be certain to follow the regulations regarding slot limits or impose some on yourself. If the population you're fishing is a healthy one with abundant numbers of fish of all sizes, the bass you keep should be between 12 and 15 inches in length. Smaller and larger fish should all be released. If the population is in poor shape or if you don't know its status, release all you catch.

For those who would like a wall mount, there is an acceptable alternative to killing the fish. Quickly measure its length and girth then take the information to a taxidermist who specializes in replica mounts. It helps if you have a picture of the fish, but it isn't necessary. The mount outlasts the real thing and, far better, the fish lives on to thrill you again. If you're curious about weight, simply multiply the length by the square of the girth and divide the result by 800.

Pass It On

How can we measure the value of sharing someone's first catch? What is it worth to see their eyes when they land their first bass or when they remove a fly from the vise that took shape under your watchful eye? Priceless.

All too soon we'll be sharing our secret haunts with the next generation. Whether or not they value and respect those places as we do depends entirely upon the quality of their mentors. In the final analysis, it's completely up to us.

We remember our mentors quite well. They imparted their knowledge, values, ethics, and skills so gently it was years before we realized how much we'd learned from them. That approach allows the student to provide the motivation.

Whatever your skill level, you have something to offer. Share your knowledge, experiences, enthusiasm, love of the places fish live, and ethics. After all, you don't need to be an expert to teach a kid to have fun fly-fishing for largemouth bass.

Like many other warmwater fly fishers, our home waters have always been bass waters. We learned fly-casting over mucky ponds, the art of the drift in muddy rivers, and the nuances of presentation among the branches of mossy brush piles. We love the places we fish as much as the bass they deliver, so our commitment to the sport of bassin' with fly rods involves no temporary fascination, but rather, a lifelong passion for the places bass live.

We've read so little in the last five decades about the beautiful places bass live it would seem writers hold those waters in low regard. We tend to focus only on where-to and how-to; somehow our appreciation of the largemouth's environment falls victim to limited space between the first page and back cover. Perhaps it's assumed bass water is commonplace and needs no more description than naming its region and defining its structure. In reality, ponds, streams, and lakes are so diverse in appearance and character that, although we have a concept of the expression, "commonplace," we just can't apply it. The idea that warmwater fish live in less picturesque, less wild, less romantic places because some were created by men with earth-moving equipment overlooks their unforgettable beauty.

Casting to pockets in the cattails is as good an excuse as there will ever be for spending time with great blue herons and calling bobwhites. On prairie ponds at sunset, the "magic time" of fabled summer bucket-mouths, poppers, and sudden stillness bathed in orange light, swallows capture insects near the shimmering surface. Quiet lake coves offer retreats into seclusion where cautious whitetails watch from the shadows. Pale bulrushes in spring's morning fog and dingy whitecaps beneath the folds of November's clouds have borne witness to our bass fishing lessons.

Before we case our rods, we store the memories of hazy summer mornings, the sounds of water on rocks, the soft whispers of dry leaves, and the musty smell of riverbanks to nourish our spirits and sustain us until we can return.

Bibliography

Bauer, Erwin A. *The Bass Fisherman's Bible.* Garden City, New York: Doubleday & Company, Inc. 1961

Brooks, Joe. *The Complete Book of Fly Fishing. Outdoor Life,* U.S.A. 1968

Dalrymple, Byron. *Modern Book of the Black Bass.* New York: Winchester Press. 1972

Hauptman, Cliff. *The Fly Fisher's Guide to Warmwater Lakes.* New York: Lyons & Burford, 1995

Henshall, James Alexander. *Book of The Black Bass.* Cincinnati, Ohio: R. Clarke & Co. 1881

Kilgour, D. Marc and Robert W. McCauley. "Effect of Air Temperature on Growth of Largemouth Bass in North America" Transactions of the American Fisheries Society. 119:276-281, 1990. American Fisheries Society. 1990

Kreh, Lefty. *Fly Fishing For Bass: Smallmouth, Largemouth and Exotics.* Birmingham, Alabama: Odysseus Editions, Inc. 1993

Leonard, J. Edson. *Flies.* Cranbury, New Jersey: A. S. Barnes and Company, Inc. 1950

Livingston, A. D. *Flyrodding for Bass.* Philadelphia & New York: J. B. Lippincott Company. 1976

Livingston, A. D. *Fishing for Bass.* Philadelphia & New York: J. B. Lippincott Company. 1974

Lucas, Jason. *Lucas on Bass Fishing.* New York: Dodd, Mead & Co., Inc. 1962

McClane, A. J., ed. *McClane's Standard Fishing Encyclopedia.* New York: Holt, Rinehart and Winston. 1965

Meyer, Deke. *Float Tube Fly Fishing.* Portland, Oregon: Frank Amato Publications. 1989

Meyer, Deke. *Flyfishing Inflatables.* Portland, Oregon: River Graphics. 1999

Nixon, Tom. *Fly Tying and Fly Fishing for Bass and Panfish.* Cranbury, New Jersey: A. S. Barnes & Co. Inc. 1968

Reynolds, Barry and John Berryman. *Beyond Trout: a Flyfishing guide.* Boulder, Colorado: Johnson Publishing Company. 1995

Sosin, Mark and Bill Dance. *Practical Black Bass Fishing.* New York: Crown Publishers, Inc. 1974

Sosin, Mark and Lefty Kreh. *Practical Fishing Knots.* New York: Lyons & Burford, Publishers. 1991

Stewart, Dick and Farrow Allen. *Flies for Bass and Panfish.* Intervale, New Hampshire: Northland Press. 1992.

Tryon, Chuck and Sharon. *Figuring Out Flies.* Rolla, Missouri: Ozark Mountain Fly Fishers. 1990

Waterman, Charles F. Black *Bass & the Fly Rod.* Harrisburg, Pennsylvania: Stackpole Books. 1993

Whitlock, Dave. L. L. Bean *Flyfishing for Bass Handbook.* New York: Nick Lyons Books. 1988.

Index

Index

Authors' Biography

Terry and Roxanne Wilson first shared their warmwater fly-fishing knowledge in an article about bluegill fly-fishing in *Fishing and Hunting Journal* published in the late 1980s. Practical advice about fly-fishing for largemouth bass followed

in *Flyfishing & Tying Journal*, *Bassmaster*, *The Flyfisher*, *Flyfishing Quarterly*, *Warmwater Fly Fishing*, *Popular Fly Fishing*, *Ontario Out of Doors*, *Thicket's Hunting and Fishing Journal*, *Outdoor Guide*, and many other magazines. They have written nearly a hundred warmwater fly-fishing articles for outdoor publications. Frank Amato Publications, Inc. released their first book, *Bluegill Fly Fishing and Flies*, in 1999.

Terry's original flies for largemouth bass, bluegills, and smallmouth bass have been featured in *Flyfishing & Tying Journal*, *Fly Fish America*, *Warmwater Fly Fishing*, and *Popular Flyfishing*.

The Wilsons have promoted catch-and-release warmwater fly-fishing throughout their writing career.

They are members of the Smallmouth Alliance and are active life members of the Federation of Fly Fishers. They were presented with the Federation's Don Harger Memorial Award in 1996 for their contributions to the sport of fly-fishing.

Terry and Roxanne Wilson have enjoyed warmwater fly-fishing together for nearly thirty-five years. Their home waters are the reservoirs and streams of the lakes region in southwest Missouri's Ozark Mountains.